D0861019

CONFESSIONS OF A POACHER

Jim Connell 1852–1929
From *Socialism and the Survival of the Fittest* (1897)
Courtesy The Working Class Movement Library,
Manchester, England

CONFESSIONS
OF A POACHER

JIM CONNELL

with an Afterword by
FRANCIS DEVINE

THE LILLIPUT PRESS
in association with
THE JIM CONNELL MEMORIAL COMMITTEE

First published 2004 by
THE LILLIPUT PRESS
62–63 Sitric Road, Arbour Hill,
Dublin 7, Ireland
www.lilliputpress.ie
Original publication, London 1901

Copyright © The Lilliput Press
and the Jim Connell Memorial Committee, 2004

All rights reserved. No part of this publication may
be reproduced in any form or by any means
without the prior permission of the publisher.

A CIP record for this title is available from
The British Library.

1 3 5 7 9 10 8 6 4 2

ISBN 1 84351 057 X

This book was produced with assistance from

Set in 11 on 14 pt Dante
Printed by Colour Books Ltd., Dublin

CONTENTS

I

"SPEAK OF ME AS I AM"

"I am as free as Nature first made man,
Ere the base laws of servitude began,
When wild in woods the noble savage ran."

IN THESE WORDS Dryden aptly expresses what the poacher feels. The hunting instinct developed by generations of savage ancestors has surely been transmitted to my companions and to myself; and we, by our adventures on field and hillside, illustrate the lives of those who have gone before. Endowed by Nature with strong and active bodies, we feel an irresistible impulse to find an outlet for our sporting instincts and physical energy. We do not contend that our pursuits are governed by the highest moral considerations; but we plead that, considering the few opportunities for enjoyment to be found in this country of monopolised land and soul-killing competition, we have led lives more unselfish and far more enjoyable than that of the average man.

Many books have been written on poaching, but, as far as I am aware, not one by anybody who has understood the subject. A practical poacher could tell at a glance that most of the adventures related never occurred. Here the case is different. I have taken a principal part in nearly all the events described, and can guarantee the correctness of the rest, so that I give to the public in these pages an actual picture of poaching as it is followed in the pursuit of fur and feathers—a picture marred by no exaggeration, and for which I need offer no apology.

Many worthy persons consider that the poacher is but an ordinary thief. As some of my readers may hold that view, I will quote a few opinions which ought to produce a very different impression. A legal writer says: "By the very nature of the case, wild animals cannot be made the subject of that absolute kind of ownership which is generally signified by the term property. The substantial basis of the law of property is physical possession—the actual power of dealing with things as we see fit; and we can have no such power over animals in a state of nature."

A Select Committee of the House of Commons inquired into the Game Laws in 1845–46. The following is taken from its report:—

"Your Committee finds an anomalous species of property, for the protection of which a severe criminal code is in operation, preserved with the most passionate ardour by a considerable number of the landed proprietors of the country; while all other classes regard game as no property, or hold the special laws enacted for its protection to be mischievous and unjust."

Again: "The farmer, whose crops are injured by the game bred on his farm, over which he has no control, disregards infractions of the law, and not infrequently looks upon the poacher as his best friend. His labourers partake of their master's feelings, and deem the taking of game at least an innocent if not a meritorious act. Unlike other offences, it is in evidence that volunteer prosecutors and witnesses against poachers are almost unknown, and that it is by the testimony of gamekeepers and watchers that convictions take place."

Again: "The same passion for sport which animates the game preserver leads the poacher into his perilous course of life. All the witnesses describe poachers as men of shrewdness and activity superior to the average agricultural labourers."

Another Select Committee sat on the Game Laws in 1873. In giving evidence before it, Mr. E. Ellice, M.P., said that the public both of England and Scotland did not look upon a breach of the Game Laws as a moral offence at all, and that a man who would take hares would not steal a fowl on any account. Mr. Hayward, farmer, of Suffolk, said to the same Committee:

"There is a parish near me called Westleton, where there is a regular gang of poachers, and has been for the last thirty years. The farmers in the neighbourhood do not dislike there being such a gang. We call them the 'farmer's friends'. Those men never commit robberies. There is no parish where there is less depredation on property than in that parish."

Mr. Richardson, another witness, said:

"Many men have been committed for offences under the Game Laws who do not themselves consider it a crime, and who would blush to commit a robbery even to the extent of a turnip."

Similar statements might easily be multiplied. As Mr. Barclay, Sheriff of Perthshire, once said, the landlords have "put game, which is not property, in a higher scale than property." Moreover, they constantly feed their game, which cannot be prevented from wandering, at other people's expense. To make the case for the poacher's character complete, we have only to mention a fact which is known to everybody where game is preserved, that the game-preserving landlord is almost always ready to make the poacher a gamekeeper. The high authority on sport, "Stonehenge" says of such men:

"It is only when worn out as poachers that they think of turning round and becoming keepers."

II

EARLY DAYS

I WAS BARELY EIGHT years old when I first saw a hare chased and caught by a greyhound. The sight was quite unexpected, and I well remember how it threw me into such a state of excitement that for some moments I could not speak. Hares were scarce in the part of the country in which I then lived, and although I longed for a repetition of the experience, nearly four years passed before I saw another course run.

By then my family had removed to a different district, where hares were almost as plentiful as blackberries. We lived in a spot bordered on one side by the Bog of Allan, and on the other by the Slieve Bloom Mountains. In both hares were to be counted by the thousand, and it need hardly be added that the country between, some two miles across, was always well stocked. The bog, too, was frequented by wild ducks, wild geese, and grouse; and every half mile there tumbled down from the mountains streams which swarmed with trout, and, during part of the year, with salmon also.

Many a happy day have I spent along the banks of these streams. A party of three or four boys would start from home about nine o'clock in the morning. Equipped with an eel spear, a couple of long rods with snares attached, a long-handled landing net, and sometimes a pail for teeming purposes, we would walk for miles along the banks, and when we felt hungry, picnic on the fish we had caught.

One of the first illegal acts which I committed was suggested by a policeman. A member of the Royal Irish Constabulary, named Brennan, pointed out how one of the mountain streams could be diverted from its channel. Those streams seldom run straight downhill. Much more frequently, during at least part of their course, they bend round it. By selecting a favourable spot and digging a channel on the lower side of the stream, the water may be turned out on the field, and the bed for a long distance below that point left wholly or in great part dry.

We were in the habit of drawing nets across the stream at three or four points, knowing well that when fish find a stream running dry they generally hurry down with it as fast as they can swim. Thus it happened that after diverting the water we invariably found a large number of fish collected behind each of the nets. Some of the streams had rather deep pools, and these we were often obliged to teem. It was not uncommon to make a bag of a hundred in a day in this manner.

Spearing eels was another favourite diversion. In the mud bottomed streams issuing from the bog eels were plentiful, and anybody acquainted with such places will know that it is always easy to see where an eel lies buried in the mud by the mark he leaves in going down. In the course of a day's ramble one handy man may secure fifty in this manner.

In one of those streams, which ran into the Shannon, I have seen young salmon so plentiful that it is hardly an exaggeration to say that from an elevated spot on the bank ten thousand might be counted. To catch these was an easy matter. We only had to take a lidless basket with a handle across it, attach a rope to the handle, throw the basket to the other side of the stream, and haul it quickly across.

At this early period of my life I became familiar with a gun. Long before I was strong enough to raise an ordinary gun to my shoulder I learned to shoot with an ancient cavalry carbine of small size. A companion of mine named Shepherd and I used to crib eggs from our mothers with which to buy powder. We generally made our own shot. When we had secured a pound of powder we always treated ourselves to a day's sport, in the course of which we blazed away at grouse, partridge, snipe, and, indeed, anything and everything that turned up. The quickness of sight and accuracy of aim acquired then have stood me in good stead since.

There was always available a large gun of the Queen Anne type, with which we used to shoot rabbits at long range by resting it on a stump. It was a six bore, and would kill at a great distance.

My friend the policeman taught us how to turn this to account in another way. In the autumn wild geese came up in flocks from the bog after nightfall, spreading themselves over the stubble fields in search of grain.

Towards evening we took a very long rope, or ball of string, and, selecting a clump of bushes or a spot in a ditch where we could conceal ourselves, we made fast one end of the string, and drew the other away some two hundred yards over a level part of the field, until it was extended in a perfectly straight line. Along this, for about twelve inches on either side, we shook barley or oats. At the end selected for hiding we drove two or three pegs into the ground to indicate the exact direction of the line, and there we took our places at nightfall, armed with the Queen Anne, and sometimes one or two other guns, charged with slugs and shot.

As soon as one of the geese discovered the corn he immediately gave tongue, and in a very short time the whole flock were ranged along the line, and busy with the bait. They all gabbled more or less, and when we thought the right moment had arrived we fired the guns. I have seen as many as eight fall to a single discharge. This scheme will only work on dark nights, as wild geese have a habit of flying over the fields on which they wish to alight, and if they see anybody they sheer off.

We also tried another plan for catching wild geese, at the bidding of the policeman. We pegged down a line on a stubble field, and strewed some corn along it. Attached to the line, every two yards or so, were eel-hooks baited with bread or dough. The corn was not too plentifully strewn, and when it began to grow scarce the geese took the bait.

The noise they made revealed to us how matters stood, and on going towards them a strange sight presented itself. The night was rather bright, and so we could see all that happened. Five geese were hooked, and on seeing us approach they attempted to fly away. At first they could not rise, but the line was fastened by only two pegs, one at either end, and repeated tugs drew these out of the soft ground. Then the geese rose.

For a moment we thought they were lost to us, but it soon appeared that they could not agree as to the route they should take. Whilst one wanted to visit New York, another was equally determined to take shelter in Timbuctoo, and a third made for St. Petersburgh.

When they found they could not go in the directions they desired, they all suddenly reversed their routes, and this caused an entanglement which brought them to the ground with great force. Some were stunned by the fall, and all were easily captured. After this first experiment we made an improvement by attaching each hook to a separate peg, driven well into the ground, and in this way we caught a large number of geese in the course of the winter. I would not, however, advise anybody to pursue this plan, for it is cruel and unsportsmanlike.

Before I was fifteen years old I became an object of hatred to a gamekeeper named Paddy Brophy. This was the result of frequent incursions which I made into the preserve which he guarded. It lay within easy reach, and it always held plenty of hares. Shooting, or otherwise catching geese, ducks, or grouse was simply a way of varying my pleasure; my permanent delight lay in chasing hares.

No one acquainted with country life will need to be told that dogs are extremely fond of hunting, and that they will always follow anybody who has once shown them good sport. At the time in question I was on such excellent terms with every dog within a radius of two miles of my home that I had only to whistle in order to make him follow me.

My canine comrades were of all breeds and sizes, and numbered about twenty. They ranged from terrier to mastiff, and there were no two of them which uttered the same cry. Of course there were four or five greyhounds, which always hunted silently. It was thus no uncommon occurrence for me to enter Paddy Brophy's preserve accompanied by a dozen dogs, and the reader can imagine the hubbub which was raised when a hare bolted.

Paddy was quite sixty years old, and, like most keepers, extremely lazy. I am inclined to think that I was the only poacher who caused him any inconvenience. He repeatedly swore that when he caught me he would half kill me, but at that age I was somewhat difficult to catch, and so the punishment never came off. To prosecute me was out of the question, for game prosecutions were unknown in that part of the country.

On one occasion he sought my father, and remonstrated with him.

"If," said he, "your son would take a hare or two quietly I would not care a rap, but he never comes on my ground without bringing a pack of dogs with him which alarm the whole parish."

My father promised to reprimand me, and for a month or two I lay low.

In the summer months I have penetrated the Slieve Bloom Mountains so far as to find it impossible to return the same day, and so have slept on the hills all night. There was a cavern about fifteen miles from my home which was occasionally used by illicit distillers for the manufacture of poteen. To this I always paid a visit when I found myself at all near it, and if there was any whisky in the place, invariably encountered company more jovial than elevating. Whether it contained whisky or not, it was always a convenient place for resting or sleeping, and many a sound nap have I enjoyed there.

So passed the seven happiest years of my life. At the age of nineteen I removed to Dublin, and hard work and want of opportunity for a long time banished all thoughts of sport. In course of years I found my way to London, and there easier circumstances and proximity to well-stocked preserves excited afresh the desires of earlier days. The companions whose names are mentioned in the following confessions were not all encountered at once. The names given are fictitious, but the persons behind them will be easily recognised by all acquainted with the subject and the districts dealt with.

III

THE KING OF THE POACHERS

HYDE, A PRINCIPAL actor in these exploits and adventures, who is called by his acquaintances the "King of the Poachers" is now about sixty years old. He was born in mid Kent of poor parents, and was one of a numerous family. His father never received more than ten shillings a week as wages, and it is obvious that this did not provide the family with much besides bread. Indeed, for years their only luxury was an occasional rabbit or hare, which was generally caught by the subject of our sketch. From a very early age he has been an intense lover of nature; and so observant and reflective is he that not only in the matter of game, but as regards ants, beetles, and insects and birds generally, he has accumulated a stock of knowledge which would do credit to a naturalist of the first rank. In addition to this he has the artistic instinct powerfully developed. Whenever he has lived for any length of time in one house, he has ornamented it with rustic woodwork so cleverly as to excite general admiration. I had not known him long before I had an insight into this side of his character. The third or fourth time I went out with him we were accompanied by about eight others, and rode in a brake which we had hired for the night. Soon after daybreak we reached the edge of a plateau overlooking the village of Oxted. Hyde called on the driver to stop, and informed us that for forty years he had never missed an opportunity of witnessing the rising of the sun from this spot. He told us that his first sight of sunrise from there was accidental, and that he was so much struck by the beauty of the scene that he ever afterwards went out of his way to enjoy a repetition of the picture. In spite of the grumbling of one or two of the party, who were more intent on business than on beauty, we loitered for half-an-hour and saw a picture which I, at least, can never forget.

Hyde was endowed with a magnificent constitution, which almost placed him above fatigue. After the hardest day's work an hour on a sofa refreshed him so much that he could walk all night if necessary. He was small (five feet six in height), but very strong, and as active as a cat. He could readily vault over anything which he could reach with even one hand, and up to the age of thirty-six he never met a man who could outrun him. Yet this man at the age of twenty-two had never earned more than nine shillings a week. Compare this lot with that of the shrivelled members of the crutch and toothpick brigade, who habitually spend more than nine shillings (which they have never earned) on a dinner.

Hyde was a poacher at the age of ten, and remained in his native place until he had turned twenty-two. By that time he had been fined and become known to the keepers, and this made it very difficult for him to obtain employment. The end of it was that he left that part of the country and relied more and more on poaching for a living. He made himself acquainted with the habits of the animals he hunted to an extraordinary extent, and it is safe to say that there is probably no contrivance for catching wild animals known to the trappers or hunters of the American forests with which he is not familiar. It is this mastery over his art, combined with a bold and resolute heart, and a capacity for outwitting game-watchers and policemen, which has gained for him the title by which he is known—The King of the Poachers.

Hyde is never tired of saying that the part of his work which he likes best is catching hares by means of dogs. He does occasionally trap or snare a hare for pot-boiling purposes, but his delight lies in coursing them. This he considers the only true form of sport. Needless to say he has had many first-rate dogs in his time, and the care he bestowed on their training would appear incredible to the ordinary man. But a well-trained lurcher means a living to the poacher, and the pursuit can be followed with more safety in that way than in any other. I have myself taken a puppy, bred in the right way, to Hyde, and have seen him offered six pounds for it. After a little hesitation he refused to sell. "No," said he, "I lived seven winters on my last dog, and I'll live longer on this." That same animal can now "do everything but talk". Increasing age has made its master somewhat feeble, and so the burden of supporting the family falls almost wholly on the dog.

Of all the dogs he has ever kept, Hyde singles out for special eulogium an animal named "Pop". An incident in the career of this dog brings out so clearly Hyde's true character that I cannot do better than relate it. Pop was three-fourths greyhound, and the remaining fourth was a mixture of old English sheepdog and bull. Hyde obtained him as a pup, and he was catching rabbits before he was nine months old. For nearly eleven years he accompanied Hyde in all his expeditions. He always did exactly as directed. He worked to a net, or snares, or caught his game by fair running, just as his master ordered. He was just as ready to fight as to hunt, and many a time has he extricated his master from an embarrassing position by attacking the keepers who were trying to capture him. Keepers' dogs he invariably fought, and conquered if allowed. Between man and dog a friendship grew up which was so deep seated that even now when Hyde talks about him tears come into his eyes. The life of a dog is short. About the ninth season poor Pop's speed was seen to have diminished sadly, and soon after his eyesight failed. His nose remained as good as ever, but he was soon found to be useless for poaching purposes, and his master ceased taking him out. Pop thus became a burden on the family he had so long helped to maintain. Mrs. Hyde, not being given to sentiment, ventured to suggest that he should be destroyed, but this threw her husband into such a terrible rage that she never alluded to the matter again.

Three years passed, during which Pop rested on his laurels. He enjoyed the reward of a well-spent life, but continued to grow old and lazy. At length Hyde had a long and serious illness. It came on him in the month of August, and he had not quite recovered by the first of December. Fearing that the night air might cause a relapse, he dared not even poach. In that year there were several weeks, frost and snow before Christmas, and the result was that Hyde was so reduced in circumstances that in Christmas week he had nothing to eat but bread and water. The dog license, costing seven and sixpence, had to be taken out early in the new year, and where the money was to come from he did not know. The police were always very hard on him. After much painful consideration he concluded that the old dog could not live much longer, and that on the whole the best thing to do was drown him. And so one morning he told his wife that he was going to drown Pop. She did not offer any violent opposition, and he then procured a piece of rope and started off for a pond about a mile distant, accompanied by his old friend. Arrived at the brink, he attached one end of the rope to the dog's collar and the other to a large stone, and threw both as far as he could into the water. They disappeared from sight, and, turning sharply, Hyde walked away. He had not gone more than thirty yards, however, when, impelled by an irresistible desire to have another look, he hastily returned. Then he perceived that he had mistaken the depth of the pond, and left too much string between the dog and the stone. Pop was struggling and splashing, with his nose above water. Finding the scene too painful to witness, Hyde walked away again, and this time remained some minutes. When he returned there was no splashing, and he thought at first that all was over. But he soon perceived that the animal had now learned to float. When the dog caught sight of his master he gave vent to a piteous yelp (the first he had uttered) and recommenced struggling. This was too much for Hyde. Without divesting himself of a stitch he lunged into the water, which was shoulder high, and, grasping the cord drew dog and stone to the bank. The cord was soon unfastened, and the liberated Pop, after several vigorous shakings, executed a race round the field, in which he displayed better form than he had shown for years. As the water was icy cold, Hyde started for home at a run. When he arrived there, accompanied by Pop, and with teeth chattering, Mrs. Hyde naturally stared and inquired what was the matter. Whilst rapidly divesting himself of his clothes Hyde emitted a volley of oaths, and ended by declaring that the first person who dared to suggest that Pop should be destroyed would feel the full weight of his vengeance. Quite in vain did Mrs. Hyde point out that nobody *had* suggested such a thing, at least lately. In language more forcible than elegant he intimated that the idea must never again be entertained under his roof.

Some of the neighbours had noticed Hyde returning in his wet clothes, and in the course of the day the facts leaked out, and were talked about. In the evening the story reached a jolly company at a neighbouring public house, to whom Hyde was well known. A plate was passed round, and a couple of pounds collected. Next day Hyde was presented with a dog license, and Mrs. Hyde with the balance.

The wetting did not injure Pop in the least, but he put his master to very little further expense. One morning in the following summer he ate a hearty breakfast, and was found dead in his bed in the afternoon.

IV

A POACHER'S POLITENESS

IN THE SPRING of 1892 Cardiff and I had each a greyhound puppy which we wanted to try. Trying young greyhounds, that is, testing their speed and cleverness in turning and catching, is an easy matter to rich people who have land and hares of their own, or who can afford to pay for trial after trial, which generally cost a guinea each, until the value of the dog has been ascertained beyond doubt.

As Cardiff and I had no land or hares, and no guineas to waste, we resolved to utilise another man's hares, feeling strongly that the practice in running which we gave them would help to keep the dogs in a state of efficiency by the time they were required by their owner; and though it was slightly past the coursing season, we did not hesitate to break the rules for once.

It was very necessary that our dogs should be tried, for they were now over a year old, and were probably as good as they ever would be. To keep a greyhound intended for legitimate coursing is both troublesome and expensive. He has to be carefully fed and exercised, and if he is valueless the sooner the fact is ascertained the better. Of course, it often happens that the worst dog for public coursing is the best for poaching purposes, and we generally turned our wastrels to good account; but a greyhound which can win cups and stakes for his owner on a public coursing field is a little fortune in himself.

Our plan was to breed a litter every year, keep them in the orthodox manner until they were fit to try, and if they turned out useless, give them away or make them keep themselves.

One Saturday night towards the end of April we took the last train from London, and reached the abode of our friend Hyde soon after midnight. We were accompanied by Coke and Riverhead, and carried two or three bottles of whisky. Hyde's house was in darkness, but a knock soon brought him to the door, and he welcomed us, lighted a fire, and set a kettle of water on to boil. A liberal allowance of hot whisky banished all thoughts of sleep, and during its consumption we explained the object of our visit.

Young greyhounds are rather stupid in relation to their work. If slipped at a hare in a field containing bushes or even tufts of grass, they either do not see it at all or else soon lose sight of it. It is therefore very important to try them where there is nothing to obstruct the view, and if possible on flat ground. Whether they see the hare or not, if they once get loose and see other dogs running, they will in all probability run until they are quite exhausted, so that a second trial on the same day is quite valueless.

All this was well known to us, and after some discussion it was unanimously agreed that we should visit on this occasion a certain plain, about six miles distant, where the fields were very large. It was agreed further that we should arrive there not later than five o'clock in the morning, an hour at which we should probably not be disturbed.

We started in good time, leading the dogs, and taking with us several old dogs with which to try the young ones. Walking briskly, we had covered about four miles by daybreak, and the morning was beautifully warm and clear. I happened to be walking in front, and, looking over a hedge which ran parallel with the road, I noticed a number of rabbits on a field. I immediately bobbed down my head and waited for the others to come up.

After a moments consultation we agreed to loose the old dogs and let them try for a rabbit.

My Nellie instantly dashed through the hedge, followed by the others, and in a moment two rabbits were captured. But there must have been two hundred on the field, all of which by this time were safe in their burrows in the side of a sandy hillock.

Someone presently remarked that it was a pity we had no ferret with us to make the rabbits bolt, whereupon Hyde said that he knew where there were ferrets, and not far away. He pointed out a house a few hundred yards off, explained that it was a keeper's lodge, and said that there were plenty of ferrets in hutches in the garden behind it. Cardiff at once volunteered to fetch one. He ran towards the place, and in about ten minutes returned with two.

Muzzles were soon made of twine, and the ferrets turned into the burrows. Soon the rabbits began to bolt, and, needless to say, the dogs caught them as fast as they came out. In a few minutes we had a dozen, which was as many as we desired, for we expected to get some hares later on, and did not wish to overload ourselves. The ferrets kept coming out after the rabbits, and the order was given to pick them up.

When that had been done the question arose—what shall we do with them? Cardiff said, addressing Hyde, "Will you have them, Jimmy?" Hyde replied, "No, I have got six already, and can always borrow one when I want it." Then someone said, "Turn them loose here." To this Hyde replied, "If you do that they will kill every rabbit in the place, and we may want to come here again." Cardiff remarked, "That is true. I will put them back where I found them."

The road along which we had come was almost perfectly straight for the last mile or more, and so it continued for about a quarter of a mile farther, bending off then sharply to the left. A footpath branched off almost opposite to where we stood, passed the door of the keeper's house, and ran into the road beyond the bend, thus enclosing a triangle. Cardiff suggested that instead of going round the road with the others I should take the footpath with him, so that I might hold his dogs whilst he went into the garden with the ferrets. I agreed, and in a few minutes the place was reached, and the ferrets replaced safely in their hutch.

When, however, Cardiff came out of the garden, instead of walking away he, to my astonishment, seized the door knocker and delivered a series of sledge-hammer raps, loud enough to awaken the dead. Almost immediately a man attired in a night-shirt only put his head out the upstairs window, and said in a voice which showed him to be still half asleep, "what do you want?" The following conversation then ensued.

CARDIFF: "Oh, don't disturb yourself. I only want to thank you for the loan of those ferrets."
KEEPER: (with a sleepy, stupid expression on his face). "What ferrets?"
CARDIFF: "Your ferrets."
KEEPER: "Where are they?"
CARDIFF: "In the hutch in the garden."
KEEPER: "What do you mean?"
CARDIFF: "Well, let me explain. We were coming up the road yonder (pointing to it), and we saw some rabbits on a field. We could not catch them without ferrets, and so we borrowed a couple of yours. I have now put them back in the hutch where I found them, and I want to thank you for the use of them."
KEEPER: (after a pause, and with face now brightening up). "Wait there till I come down."
CARDIFF: "Oh, don't trouble to come down. We have a long distance to go and cannot wait."
KEEPER: (pulling in his head). "Oh, wait a moment."
CARDIFF: "Hi! hi! halloo!"
KEEPER: (putting his head out again). "Well?"
CARDIFF: "Look here, old boy. Take my advice and don't come down, for if you do, by jingo you'll repent it."

We then walked off at a steady pace, and saw no more of the keeper.

V

FOOLSCAPS FOR PHEASANTS

For some years I was a member of one of the London vestries, and in discharging the duties of that office neces sarily came into contact with some men of good means. One evening about nine o'clock I was a little surprised by a visit from one of the most amiable and intelligent of my colleagues, who said that he desired a private—a very private interview. I took him into a quiet room, locked the door, and listened to his story.

He was then over sixty, and had been a shopkeeper in a large way since early youth. He had, in fact, during most of the time run nearly a dozen shops. His family was now scattered and provided for, and finding himself growing feeble, he had determined to retire from business, and had already built himself a very pretty villa, which stood in about three acres of land in a southeastern suburb. The ground was laid out in lawn and garden, and he was now doing his best to make the place attractive. His wife was a great lover of birds, and had a special fancy for a spacious and well-stocked aviary in the open air; and to gratify her wish he had enclosed with wire-netting a space about fifty yards long by ten yards wide, which contained some small trees, and turned into it a large number of birds of different sorts.

He had, however, been quite unable to procure any pheasants. Dead ones he could, of course, buy anywhere, but those who had live ones refused to sell them. This I could quite believe, and he told me that in the course of his inquiries he had been recommended to apply to me as one who would be likely to procure some specimens. He hoped his request would give no offence, and begged me to do what I could to help him.

I assured him that, although a little amused, I was not at all offended, but expressed a doubt as to my ability to be of any use. I promised, however, to speak to some of my poaching acquaintances, and let him know the result. He asked me what price poachers usually charged for live pheasants, but as I was unable to tell him, he said that he would willingly pay double the price of dead ones, and that he would take six. With this he left me.

It happened that about ten days later, on a Sunday, I found myself within three miles of the residence of our old friend Hyde, and I thereupon resolved to walk across to his cottage and speak to him about these pheasants. I reached his place about two o'clock in the afternoon, and told him my business, asking him if he could procure what was wanted.

"Certainly, I can," he said.

I then asked when he would be likely to get them, as, if my friend should inquire, I should like to be ready with an answer.

Hyde replied, "Oh, I think I'll get them this afternoon. Anyhow, I will have a try, and you can come along with me if you like." I agreed, and he then called on Mrs. Hyde to furnish us with a cup of tea before we started.

Whilst tea was being brewed I noticed that Hyde took a couple of newspapers and cut them into about eight-inch squares. He then twisted these round his fingers into little bags of extinguisher shape, or such as are used by the keepers of sweet-stuff shops to wrap lozenges in. He then stuck the bags into one another, so that they could be carried readily without being crushed, and also placed in his pockets some handfuls of barley and an iron implement like a thick sharp-pointed poker. He then took from a cupboard a bottle with a wooden cap, through which the handle of a brush was passed, of the sort which is used in most offices for holding paste. This bottle, instead of gum, contained birdlime. After tea we started.

We walked about three miles, mostly across fields, and at length reached a road which was very little used, and fairly well known to me. Moving along it for some distance we came to a gate on the right, opening into a field some two hundred yards wide with a wood at its farther side, which ran parallel with the road. Hyde directed me to sit on the gate and whistle to him if I saw any one approaching whom I considered dangerous. He then walked across the field, disturbing as he went several pheasants, which ran or flew into the wood.

When he was within twenty yards of the trees he pulled out his iron tool, dug it into the ground, and worked it round in such a manner as to widen the hole it had made. He then withdrew it and dug it in again, working it round in the same way as before. When he had made the hole large enough he placed one of the paper bags in it, dropped a few grains of barley into the cup, and by means of his brush anointed the inside with birdlime. He then moved on some three or four yards, made another hole, and lined it in exactly the same way. Proceeding thus, always parallel with the wood, he repeated the operation until his paper bags were exhausted.

For the information of the uninitiated, it may be mentioned here that most pheasants are, during some part of their lives, fed by hand. It follows that although they will run away from a stranger, yet if they see him lingering near their haunts, especially in a stooping posture, they keep their eyes fixed on him, and the moment he goes away they approach the place he has vacated, hoping to find food there. On the occasion of which I speak more than a dozen had emerged from the wood before Hyde had returned to the gate on which I sat.

We were not obliged to wait long for results. I watched the business closely, and this is what happened. A fine cock bird ran boldly across the grass, and dipping his head into one of the holes to get at the barley, withdrew it covered with the paper bag which the birdlime had stuck fast. He then started shaking his head with an energy which was highly amusing. He shook and shook it at a frantic rate, almost sufficient, one would have thought, to make it fly from his body. But never a hair's-breadth did the birdlimed paper move,

Despairing of getting clear in this way, he executed with lightning rapidity a number of scratches with his right foot, and a similar number with his left, but still the birdlime held the paper on. Hyde explained to me that this scratching generally only serves to rub the birdlime into the eyes, so that even if the paper be scratched off the bird cannot see.

In the space of a minute three pheasants were shaking and scratching together. I volunteered to fetch them, as I feared that the example of their misfortune might act as a warning to the others and drive them away. But Hyde knew better, and would not allow me to stir. In about ten minutes there were nine birds deprived of the use of their eyes, and shaking or scratching their heads, or moping about. As we required only six, Hyde now drew from his pocket a canvas bag, thin and porous, and walked rapidly towards them.

Two of them must, by some means or other, have got a corner of an eye open, for on Hyde's approach they ran into the wood. The other seven were soon placed in the bag, having allowed themselves to be picked up as quietly as possible.

We returned to Hyde's house by the same paths we had traversed in coming, and waited there until night fell. Then we took train to London, and very soon reached the gate of the man who had bespoken the pheasants. I waited outside whilst Hyde transacted his business. In a short time he came back to me with the price paid for the birds in his hand, which he smilingly opened— 7s.6d each, £2, 12s 6d in all.

A week or two later I met the purchaser in the street. He accosted me with, "You are just the man I want to see." He insisted on taking me to a neighbouring hotel, and, choosing a very quiet corner, he called for a bottle of champagne; and when the second measure of the sparkling wine bubbled in our glasses he said, "Now tell me how you caught those pheasants."

I described the exploit just as it had occurred, and he laughed immoderately. He said that when Hyde left the birds he directed that their heads should be washed with warm water. He added, "My wife has been washing them with warm water ever since, and they are not clean yet. We guessed that the sticky stuff must be birdlime, but wondered how on earth you got it on. However, they are very fine birds, and I am well satisfied with my bargain."

VI

A POACHER IN HIS CUPS

THE MONTH WAS September, and the weather was delightfully warm. About eight o'clock one Saturday evening Cardiff and Greenman called on me, and saying that they were going out for the night, asked me to accompany them. I hastily finished my work, and, calling the dogs, walked with them to the nearest railway station.

About ten o'clock we reached Hyde's house. He was not at home, but we learned from Mrs. Hyde that we should probably find him at "The Feathers", a public house which was close at hand. Thither we repaired, and discovered him, with a companion spirit named Yallop, enjoying a pipe and glass. We joined them, and remained until closing time.

Now, this Yallop was a remarkable man, about twenty-seven years old, tall, powerful, and full of animal spirits. He was very good-natured, and seldom lost his temper, but even the dullest could see that with his blood up he would be a dangerous antagonist. He had evidently been drinking pretty freely this evening, and was inclined to be musical and noisy.

When closing time arrived we went outside, and Yallop, addressing Hyde, said, "Jimmy, the night is just about fit" (meaning neither too bright nor too dark). "Shall we get the guns?"

Hyde replied that he was perfectly willing, and, directing us to meet them at a point about half a mile distant, the two men went off towards their homes.

The guns were soon brought out, and after walking a couple of miles along quiet roads we reached a high wooden fence enclosing a gentleman's demesne. Handing his gun to one of the company, Yallop vaulted over, and then reached for the fire-arms. We all scrambled across as best we could, and almost immediately the squeal of a rabbit told us that one of the dogs had drawn first blood.

Hyde and Yallop now began to search for pheasants. Their plan was to place themselves under a tree and bring every branch in succession between them and the brightest part of the sky. By this means they were able to see whether any birds were roosting there.

Their search, however, met with no reward: not a pheasant was to be seen. With muffled oaths they declared that the birds "must be somewhere," and travelled over a large portion of the park, looking on all sides as they went. Meantime the dogs had caught three or four rabbits, and kept working the ground in front of us.

All at once we were startled by strange noises to the right. Hissing and snorting alternated with bumps against trees and sounds as of ploughing. The rattle of chains faintly suggested to my active imagination the possible presence of an escaped lunatic. The dogs growled ominously, and alternately made spirited advances and undignified retreats. We proceeded cautiously in the direction of the noises and discovered a bull, with a complete set of harness on, and yoked to a balk of timber, which was, in fact, almost the whole trunk of a large tree. He could not move without dragging this about with him.

As we came up he was making frantic efforts to get at the dogs, which, of course, avoided him. Almost before I understood the situation he made a dash at me, and my escape, which was quite as narrow as a Spanish bull-fighting audience could desire, excited the hearty laughter of my companions.

However, the bull was impartial, and making for each in turn sent the laugh all round. We stood wondering for some time what could be the reason for compelling the animal to drag this burden about day and night, but beyond agreeing that it was not good conduct that procured his sentence, we came to no conclusion. We learned later that this bull was extremely valuable, but terribly vicious, having ripped up several horses.

At this point I could not help noticing that Yallop had lost much of the business-like seriousness which he had previously displayed. I had observed that on several occasions he retired into the shadows, but did not suspect until now that his object in doing so was to imbibe whisky from a bottle which we had given him to carry. As the outcome of a whispered consultation, we all called for a "nip", and took care that the bottle was not returned to Yallop.

After wandering about for some time longer we found ourselves at the back of the mansion itself. Here we came upon a poultry enclosure, a very extensive affair, covering more than a quarter of an acre, formed of thick wire, and in places roofed. When we reached it Yallop placed his gun on the grass, and actually began pulling it down. For a moment I was disgusted, as I believed his object was to steal the poultry, but Hyde relieved me when he pronounced it "all pure devilment".

The wire fence did not long resist Yallop's herculean strength. When he had brought down a great length of it he entered the fowl-houses, and with loud laughter and shouts chased the birds off their perches. He managed to get hold of a piece of rope, and with this he scattered the unfortunates over the lawn. Ducks, chickens, guinea-fowls, turkeys, and geese all screamed together, and Yallop's laugh was heard above all else.

In the middle of this pandemonium it suddenly occurred to me that we were dangerously near the mansion, and that a very moderate marksman could readily raise a window and bring me down. I said as much to my friend Greenman, and we prudently retired out of range.

Not until the last bird had been driven forth did Yallop desist. Then he wiped his brow with a handkerchief, and seemed satisfied. To me the most astonishing part of the performance was the absence of any disturbing element. The inhabitants of that house, numbering, as I learned afterwards, over twenty, must have been sound sleepers. In the stillness of the night the noise seemed to me sufficient to arouse the dead.

Hyde now decided that we should make for a wood about a mile distant, where, he said, we were sure to find plenty of pheasants. His decision delighted me. I had come out to do a night's poaching, and prepared to take its risks, but I shrank from the prospect of being run in for robbing a hen-roost.

Half-an-hour's walk brought us to the wood indicated by Hyde, who informed us that it was very closely watched. We got over the fence as quietly as possible, and Hyde then made his arrangements. The wood, he said, was a large one, over a mile long, and contained so many keepers that we must remain there but a very short time after firing the first shot. His plan was to secure a few birds as rapidly as possible, and then clear out. We had not proceeded many paces when we saw a light in front of us.

Hyde, who was familiar with the place, declared that it shone in one of those wooden huts or shelters which are built for the accommodation of keepers in all game preserves. He added, however, that we need feel no alarm, as the keepers frequently lighted a candle and left it burning in these places before going home to bed, in the hope of frightening poachers away. He volunteered to go on in front to ascertain whether there was anybody in the hut, and bade us remain where we stood.

Yallop was too impatient to stand still, and walked slowly after Hyde, followed by the rest of us. When we reached a point, about seventy yards from the shelter we saw that Hyde was returning. He waved his hand to us to keep back. Instead of doing so, however, Yallop pressed forward, and in a loud voice inquired if the hut was tenanted. Hyde replied quietly that there were two keepers there.

"Two of them!" repeated Yallop, in a voice that rang through the wood. "Well, Jimmy," he continued, "do you walk around and get a bird or two, and I'll stand here on guard, and if they put out their noses I'll shoot them both."

Hyde did as directed. Standing under a tree he scanned its branches, and then bang went his gun, and down tumbled two pheasants.

"Bravo, Jimmy," shouted Yallop, "get a few more. These beggars are quiet enough."

Four shots in all broke the stillness of the night, with the result that six pheasants were knocked over, and handed to my friends and myself to carry. Hyde then suddenly said: "Here's out of it."

Yallop did not move until he had delivered a parting speech to the imprisoned keepers.

"We are going now," said he, "and if you are wise you'll remain where you are. Don't follow us unless you want me to put a charge of number five into your carcasses."

As far as I could see they took his advice. Certain it is that we walked away in a leisurely manner, without interference from anybody.

After a further walk of two miles in the direction of more open country, we sat down by a brook to finish our whisky and rest the dogs. When day broke we enjoyed some good coursing, and returned with four hares, seven rabbits, and six pheasants as the result of our night's adventures.

The reader will be glad to learn that Yallop has turned over a new leaf. A strict teetotaller for over eight years, he is now the possessor of a thriving business, and although he still finds an occasional outlet for his superabundant energy in roving expeditions in the still night and the dim light of early morning, he is free from the eccentricities which characterised him in the days when he was wont to lose himself in his cups.

VII

A BATTLE IN THE DARK

THE TIME WAS about two o'clock in the morning; the place was a valley in Surrey, about a mile and a half long. Through the centre of this ran a road, from which the ground on either side sloped upwards for a distance of six hundred yards. The road, which was straight, formed the bottom of the valley, and was not enclosed with ditches or fences of any sort. The valley, in fact, did not contain a single bush. It ran east and west.

We—Cardiff, Riverhead, Greenman, and I—entered it at the western end. We seldom visited this place without catching a few hares. We turned to the right, off the road, and spread ourselves over the ground. For some days the weather had been rather wet, and the sky was covered with black clouds; still there was what Cardiff called "good dog light". For the benefit of the uninitiated, it may be mentioned that greyhounds have eyes like eagles in the daytime and like owls at night. We had not proceeded many yards over the field when a hare started in front, and soon a squeal proclaimed that first blood had been drawn. In a few minutes another and another had been added to the bag.

The bag in this case meant Greenman's overcoat. He was somewhat delicate, and was very liable to catch cold; hence many of his poaching feats were accomplished in an overcoat which reached almost to his heels. This was quite contrary to the fashion prevailing among the poaching fraternity, but Greenman was not in the habit of following examples or observing conventionalities, either good or bad. His overcoat was turned into a bag in a very simple manner. A few stitches were ripped in the lining, high up near the shoulder, and the hares dropped in between the lining and the cloth. Of course they fell to the bottom, and bumped against Greenman's heels every step he took.

As we spread ourselves over the field, it happened that I was at the extreme right of the line. As soon as we had found our places we all walked parallel with the road, and I was farthest away from it, and highest up the hill, on a course which kept me just over the brow. All the hares which were disturbed ran my way (they generally run uphill), and so my progress was somewhat slower than that of the others, in consequence of my dogs getting more courses. It took us about an hour to walk the distance, but at length the end of the valley was reached. It must not be supposed that we kept one another in sight all this time. The night was much too dark for that. However, we all knew the ground well, and knew where we were going, and it was quite understood that we should wait for one another at a certain spot.

At the farther end of the valley there was a wood which ran down to within a few yards of the road, so that in taking the line we did we made straight for it. When I was within about fifty yards of this wood I heard a voice calling out in a husky tone: "Lie down, lie down."

Never doubting that it was one of my friends who spoke, and thinking some discovery had been made, I did as directed. However, the grass was wet, and the weather was cold, and I soon grew tired of lying still. I kept my ears wide open, but could hear nothing, neither, could I see anything. The brightest part of the sky was behind me, and so it was much easier for anybody in front to see me than for me to see him. After lying for about five minutes I stood up and walked towards the wood, but had not proceeded more than ten yards when the voice again called out with greater emphasis than at first: "Lie down, lie down."

Still never doubting that it was the voice of a friend, I obeyed for the second time. I now lay so long that my teeth began to chatter with cold, and as I could not bear the situation, I stood up and walked forward. As I approached the wood I saw two men standing under the nearest trees. With the utmost confidence I walked up to them, and when I was within five or six yards discovered that they were keepers. They had evidently observed the whole gang approach, and, seeing that I was farthest from the road, resorted to this ruse in order to detach me from the others.

I was certainly taken aback, but attempted to put a good face on the matter by asking, "Which is the road to Fairchild?"

One of them answered in a quiet but determined tone, "You don't want to be told the road to Fairchild. Besides, you are not going there tonight; you are coming with us."

I mumbled something about losing my way, but was cut short by the man, who told me in a very emphatic way that I was his prisoner. I tried to parley, offered to go off their ground at once, but it was all no use. I was told that I must go straight to the nearest police station.

Then I said positively that I would not go, and that I meant to fight for my liberty. By this time I had taken the measure of the men. One was about forty years old, broad-shouldered and resolute-looking. He was evidently the man in charge, for he did all the talking. The other was about thirty, over six feet high, and of athletic build. When I announced that I would not go with them, they slowly drew apart some three or four paces. The older man raised his stick, and advanced as if to strike me. He made two or three feints, and by falling back immediately afterwards drew me a pace or two forward.

Suddenly I found myself seized from behind by the younger man, who punched the back of my head and shook me violently. His grip was like that of a vice, and I began to feel that I was securely trapped.

All at once I saw that the man in front was attacked by my dog,

Nellie. He hit her two or three times with a stick, but without uttering a cry she flew at him again and again, and compelled him to retreat rapidly. The man behind still shook and punched me, as if to inspire me with terror. I tried to turn round, but could not. At this stage he emitted an "Ugh!" which was obviously the result of pain, and, to my intense surprise, loosed his hold.

Turning towards him, I saw with delight that he was attacked by Blucher. This eased my mind immensely. I knew from experience that anybody that Blucher fought would get all he deserved, and perhaps more, and as this man carried a much lighter stick than the other, I simply turned my back on him.

I found that the shorter man had been driven back some twelve or fifteen yards by Nellie, and that he was vigorously endeavouring by kicks and blows, which seldom reached their mark, to defend himself from her teeth. Fearing that he might kill her by a heavy blow on the head, I ran forward, and without striking him, parried his blows with my stick so as to render them harmless.

Her severe attention to his legs caused him to execute a step-dance of an entirely new and original sort, which was better than many performances in the "light fantastic" line which I have paid money to witness. I soon saw that he had had enough of the business. At first he hurled at me such epithets as "Villain!" and "Scoundrel!" but soon he was fain to call out in an appealing tone: "Call her off!" Never did the fortune of war change sides more quickly.

By this time I could hear the man behind me, who was receiving the onset of Blucher, emit alternate oaths and yells. I was in no hurry to call Nellie off. My would-be captor had not yet surrendered, and I wanted a clear understanding with him before agreeing to an armistice.

At length he called out: "Are you a man, at all?" and then I stopped her. He next wanted to go to the assistance of his companion, but I barred that. For a couple of minutes we watched the fight between Blucher and his enemy, which was rapidly becoming a very one-sided affair. The keeper was getting exhausted, and Blucher was only warming to his work. He was a very big dog, weighing ninety-six pounds, and, like all lurchers, was as active as a cat. A bite from him was positively dangerous.

At first he fought cautiously, retreating instantly after each bite, and contenting himself mainly with tearing the man's clothes. At length there were few left to tear. The fellow was in tatters, like a scarecrow, and the bites began to tell. The keeper fought like a Trojan. His stick was long ago smashed to atoms, and his cuffs and kicks were quite unavailing. He began to emit piteous yells which touched my heart. The other one bawled at me: "Do you want to see the man killed?" and, indeed, I had begun to fear that his life was in danger. But I was now confronted with the problem of how to get Blucher off.

To call him was not of the slightest use. When his blood was up he would not obey me. To strike him was equally useless; he took no notice of blows. I knew that he must be pulled off by main strength, and in this line I had had a very unpleasant experience. On a former occasion, in the middle of an encounter I tried to pull him away by one of his hind-legs, but turning round with lightning-like quickness he made his fangs almost meet through my arm. Of course the poor fellow in the excitement of the moment did not know whom he was biting.

I now shouted his name three or four times as loudly as I could, to recall him to a sense of my presence, and, seizing a favourable moment, threw myself upon him, clasped him round the body, and held him. Luckily he did not bite me. He struggled to get at the keeper again, but finding I held him fast soon became quieter. I drew from my pocket a leather collar, which I buckled on his neck and held with a firm grip.

About this time the older man called out to his companion, "Bill, are you much bitten?" The answer came at once. " — — — me, I'm bitten all over." I remarked, with all the sincerity I could muster at the moment, that I was very sorry for what had occurred. I pointed out that if they had allowed me to go away quietly at first no one would have been a penny the worse, and then made for the road. All this time I kept a tight grip of Blucher's collar, as I knew from experience that if I loosed him he would probably go back and attack the man again. I soon reached the road, and walked rather briskly in the direction in which I expected to find my friends.

Before, however, I had proceeded more than two hundred yards I became aware that I was being followed, and easing my pace, discovered that my pursuers were the two men I had just left. I understood at once that their intention was to keep me in sight until we met a policeman or arrived at a village, and then have me arrested. Turning round, I walked up to them and said, "Gentlemen, if you are going this way I'll go the other," and walked past in an opposite direction. I kept my ears wide open, and in a couple of minutes discovered that they were following me again.

I saw that this must be stopped. Once more I approached them, and in language more forcible than polite, informed them that if they followed me another yard I would loose the dog and leave them subjects for the coroner. This threat had a wholesome effect. They came no farther. I now reflected that if by any chance my identity should be discovered, the charge against me would be a very serious one. The men would be sure to swear that I had set the dogs on to them. There was a police station within a mile, and they would probably give information of the occurrence there almost immediately. The news might be wired at once to all stations within a wide radius, a description of the dogs and myself circulated, and patrols put on the alert.

Taking everything into account, I thought it advisable to get off the road. I made for a quiet station from which I knew I could take an early train to London. For nine miles I traversed fields, most of them ploughed, and at length booked for a quarter of London different from the one in which I lived. Weary and hungry, I reached home before seven o'clock in the morning, and in a stretch of well-earned repose forgot the antagonists from whom I had had such a narrow escape.

For some months my friends and I avoided the scene of this encounter. News reached us, through Hyde, that the younger keeper had been severely punished, but that a fortnight's treatment by a surgeon had made him almost as good as new. By a stroke of good fortune both men found better situations within a year, and removed from that neighbourhood. When we felt assured of this we resumed our visits to the place, and never passed by without pausing to inspect the spot on which Blucher won his Waterloo.

VIII

BRIMSTONE FOR BIRDS

A MONG THOSE who took part in our expeditions was a tinker or tin-worker. He was a comparatively late accession to our strength, but we soon made most excellent use of him. Before he had been more than three times out Hyde learned the nature of his occupation, and immediately unfolded to him a scheme which, he said, he had had in his mind for years. Pheasants almost invariably roost on the lower, if not on the lowest, branches of trees, and they may be suffocated by the fumes of brimstone almost as quickly as bees.

There are difficulties however, in the way of sending the fumes up to them, even though they roost low. The gentlest breeze would make it almost impossible to affect them at a height of twenty feet. Besides, to display a light at night would almost certainly be fatal to the operations of the poacher. Hyde, however, after much cogitation, had worked out a solution of the difficulty, which he explained to our tinker comrade.

It was simply the construction of a stove of cylindrical shape, tapering towards the top, and with inlets for the air near the bottom. This was to be about eighteen inches in diameter, and to contain an arrangement for holding in position a large brimstone candle or wick, and to have a door extending its full length. The chimney was to be composed of six tubes, each fifty-four inches long and tapering towards the top, and so graduated in size that when in use they would fit over one another and form a perfect chimney. The diameter of the largest one where it fitted over the top of the stove was about fourteen inches, and that of the smallest at the top end not more than four inches. When not in use the tubes fitted into one another the reverse way, and the whole apparatus, including the stove and an ample supply of brimstone, could be placed in a sack and carried with the greatest ease by one man. By means of this pheasants could be stupefied at a height of thirty feet, and they seldom roost higher than that. When they sat lower the use of one or more sections of the chimney could be dispensed with.

Probably the greatest ingenuity was displayed in the construction of the handle. It will be easily perceived that in order to move with ease and safety an appliance some twenty-seven feet in height, a large handle, or, to be more correct, considerable leverage in the handle, was necessary. The handle which Hyde designed took the hoop form. There were, in fact, two hoops, one within the other, connected together by spokes. The outer hoop was four feet in diameter, and the inner was just large enough to fit over the top of the stove, to which it was made fast by a very simple arrangement.

The two hoops, forming the whole handle, were provided with hinges, which enabled them to be folded, and in that condition they could be placed in the sack along with the stove and its chimney. Our friend the tinker made the whole apparatus, with the exception of the handle, which was constructed by a blacksmith. Although made in spare time, it was finished in less than a fortnight, and the handicraftsman estimated that the total cost of labour and material was less than 40s.

I shall never forget the night, on which we first used it. Hyde was extremely sanguine, and looked forward with the greatest eagerness to a big haul. We were all full of curiosity, and went out in high glee. The night was dark, the moon not being up, but there was light enough to enable us to see the pheasants on the branches when we stood under the trees. We selected a spot where there was little or no undergrowth, and put our apparatus together.

We then placed it directly under two pheasants which were sleeping quietly on a branch, their heads under their wings. Hyde opened the door of the stove, and Greenman and Cardiff held a sheet of waterproof material in front whilst he put a lighted match to the brimstone, in order to shut in the light from anybody who might be about.

Immediately smoke issued from the top and encompassed the birds. In less than a minute one of them fell. He did not, as I expected, come down fluttering his wings; but fell as if quite dead, and struck the ground like a stone. A slight change in the position of the stove brought the other down a few seconds later. A move was then made to the next tree on which we could see birds, and here Fortune was very kind. Within ten minutes six more were added to our stock.

Although the weight of the apparatus was insignificant, we found that, in consequence of the height of the chimney, it required three men to move it from tree to tree with speed and safety. Two carried it and one steadied it. It did its work wonderfully well. A few pheasants, disturbed by the cracking of twigs under our feet, escaped, but as a rule fell victims to the brimstone.

We had been at work an hour and a half when a moving light warned us that there were keepers about, and as our bag was already a good one, we thought it wise to retire. When we counted our birds we found that we had forty-six.

On numberless occasions since then has that stove been brought into use. When a wedding, a dinner, or a celebration of any sort came off among our acquaintances the table never lacked smoked pheasant. Often, too, has it provided a meal for the families of the unemployed workmen to whom it has been lent.

There is a certain district (and a large one too), the name of which wild horses would not drag from me, in which the landowners have for a number of years been wondering at the lack of pheasants. No poacher's shot ever disturbs the slumbers or startles the waking moments of their keepers, and yet the birds disappear. If they could but discover the contents of a certain cart, which hails from a certain town, and meets two or three men by appointment in a certain secluded hollow, they would know that their losses are attributable to the genius of the resourceful and remorseless Hyde.

IX

A WINDFALL

THE BATTUE may be described as a very modern and very unsportsmanlike way of killing game. The old plan was to walk about in search of birds, and when they had been put up on ground of their own choosing, to shoot them if possible. The modern method is to enclose an area with hurdles or nets, converging towards a point which contains the only opening, to have the game driven by beaters to this point, round which the guns are placed, and there massacre the victims wholesale.

The gentlemen who take part in this business might just as well enter a shambles and kill a few score sheep. No skill of any sort is required, and the butchery does not even provide exercise for their limbs. But it suits lazy folk, provided they are at the same time cruel and selfish.

A good story is told of a rich cockney merchant who rented a preserve for the season, and organised a battue. A pheasant, started by the beaters, came running along towards the opening, on one side of which our friend stood with a keeper by his side. He covered the bird with his gun, and moved it so as to keep her covered as she ran. Thinking he was about to fire before the bird got on the wing, the keeper hastily interposed with, "Don't shoot, sir, whilst she runs!" "No," was the reply, "I am waiting until she stops!"

It happens that a well-known London banker keeps a preserve within a couple of miles of the residence of my friend Hyde, and, like others of his class, he has an occasional battue. On a certain morning a few years back a near neighbour of Hyde's was searching for employment in the vicinity of the banker's preserve, and was accosted by a keeper who offered him three days' work as beater. He gladly accepted the offer, and was thereupon added to a gang of about thirty youths and men who were waiting for the arrival of the guests. That day the killing was fast and furious, and the dead game were deposited in a shed in the wood, the door of which was locked when the day's work was over. On returning home in the evening the man in question happened to meet Hyde, and had a chat with him. The nature of his employment came out, and also the location of the dead game. Hyde at once decided to act. He knew the wood, and the shed, and everything about the place, and the night was dark. Fearing that the shed might be watched, he deemed it prudent to take a companion with him, and soon procured the co-operation of friend Greenman.

Equipped with two enormous sacks, they started from Hyde's cottage about midnight, and, traversing quiet paths, reached the wood and the shed. Hyde at once now drew from his pocket a screwdriver and a powerful pair of pincers. The hasp was taken off the door almost noiselessly, and the sacks filled with game. Carefully tying their mouths, the men shouldered their heavy burdens and walked towards the fence, Hyde leading the way. They met with no disturbance, but were utterly exhausted by the time they reached home. They then lay down, Hyde in bed and Greenman on a couch, until late in the morning. When they counted their booty they found that they had secured one hundred and seventy two pheasants. Some were eaten by the poachers and their families, some were presented to friends, and the remainder were sold.

When the shooting-party met next morning there were "wigs on the green". The keepers accused the hired men, and the latter accused the keepers. The banker swore like our army in Flanders. Guilt could not be brought home to anyone; but two of the keepers were discharged soon after, and everybody connected their misfortune with the disappearance of those pheasants.

Though I have no scruples as an avowed poacher, I must admit that this appropriation of game already taken, and stored for safety under lock and key, was not an honest enterprise. And while I record it as an instance of extreme audacity, I can but be glad that I took no part in an act which no sophistry can excuse or justify.

X

CLEARING THE ROUND WOOD

I WAS FOR SOME YEARS engaged in a business which compelled me to travel some twelve or fifteen miles into the country about once a week. On these journeys I generally kept my eyes open, and sometimes made discoveries which I was afterwards able to turn to good account.

On one occasion, having finished my work, I came to a railway station with the intention of returning home, but found that I had over an hour to wait for my train. As the day was cold, I adjourned to a neighbouring public house, and calling for a glass of ale, took up a newspaper.

Whilst I was thus engaged two men entered, and standing at the counter refreshed themselves with sundry drinks. The moment they came in I suspected that they were keepers, and their conversation confirmed the impression made by their velveteens. It was about the first of March, and they appeared to be keepers on two adjoining preserves, discussing various matters connected with game. I kept my eyes on the newspaper, but heard, indeed could not help hearing, the whole of the conversation.

Shooting was over for the season, and their talk ran on restocking. Among other matters one of them mentioned that sixteen pheasants had been left in the Round Wood—eight couples. This Round Wood was very well known to my friends and myself, and in fact we had many times taken rabbits in it and around it. I attached no particular importance to the information at the moment, and in due course my train arrived and I went on my way.

Just then I was extremely busy, and was hard at work in my shop when, about eight o'clock in the evening, I had a visit from Cardiff and Hyde. The latter had been in town since the morning, and reached Cardiff's place about 5 P.M., the hour at which he knew the latter would be disengaged. They had just had enough drink to make them lively, and pressed me hard to go out with them for the night. I assured them that that was utterly impossible, as I had still three hours' work to do. I told them hurriedly the conversation I had heard in the afternoon, and particularly the part which related to the Round Wood. They bade me good-night and left me. I finished my work and soon afterwards went to bed.

About four o'clock the next morning I was roused by a persistent knocking and ringing at the door. Going downstairs half dressed, I opened it and saw my two friends, Cardiff carrying across his shoulder a small sack. They came inside, and when I had lighted the gas Cardiff remarked, "How many pheasants did you say were left in the Round Wood?" I replied that their number was sixteen. He then emptied the bag on the hearthrug, and there, sure enough, lay sixteen pheasants, eight cocks and eight hens. After hearing my story they had taken the train to the station from which I had come, visited the Round Wood, and caught every one.

XI

LONG DICK

WITH CARDIFF and Riverhead I went down to Hyde's place late one Saturday night in March, but found him very unwell and unable to come out with us. He sat up, however, until about three o'clock in the morning, when we sallied forth. By daybreak we had reached some fields where we had often found hares in abundance, and we proceeded to walk them. The ground was all ploughed, and as the weather had recently been very wet, progress was difficult, for the soil was chiefly clay, and very soon we had large masses of it adhering to our boots. We persevered obstinately, but altogether without result, until we had walked almost every inch of the place without finding a single hare.

It happened that a road ran through this part of the country which was like a cutting. It was about five feet lower than the level of the surrounding fields, and had whitethorn bushes growing along it at intervals. When we made up our minds that there was no hare to be found there, we resolved to make for the road and try elsewhere. I was the first to reach it, and went down the sloping bank with a run. Up to this point we had not met or seen anybody. Indeed we had never been challenged on these fields. We knew that they were preserved, but we had heard that the keepers were old, and that, with one exception, none of them ever attempted to interfere with poachers beyond blowing their whistles.

This one exception was "Long Dick", who was a source of terror to some of us. His frame was herculean and his courage beyond question. He had frequently fought two men, and once tackled three, and although he had much the worst of this encounter, yet he professed himself ready to fight the same three again at any time. There was a feeling among poachers that, on the whole, Long Dick had better be avoided. We did not know the exact boundaries of the ground which he guarded, and long immunity had made us so careless that on this particular morning we never bestowed a thought on keepers of any sort. In this happy state of mind I entered the road, as I have said, with a run.

Imagine my surprise, then, when I saw standing before me, about three yards distant, a man nearly seven feet high. He grasped a heavy stick, as long as a broom handle, with both hands, and shook it as if he meant mischief. It flashed on me instantly that I was face to face with Long Dick. Although his name was suggestive, it had never occurred to me that he was as long as this. The man was a giant, and I felt at once that with a blow of the stick he held he could easily kill me. He held it level with his breast, and his fingers danced along it as though he were playing a flute, and was impatient to begin. I made no attempt to move, and there we stood facing each other for a few seconds which seemed like weeks, I wondering all the time whether the blow would fall above or below my left ear. Neither of us uttered a sound.

All at once I heard a footstep behind me, but did not dare to turn my head. Without a moment's hesitation Cardiff—for it was he—brushed past me, and placing himself between Long Dick and myself, addressed the latter in a strong, deep voice as follows:—

"I say what the devil do you mean by this?"

Dick replied in a voice quite as strong—

"What the devil do *you* mean?"

"What do I mean?" said Cardiff. "Why, we have walked all

these fields (swinging his arm to the left) and all those (swinging it to the right) and have not got a smell of a hare. You must be neglecting your duty. You must have allowed the poachers to kill them all off."

For a short time Dick's face was a study. Bewilderment was its predominant expression, for after all he was a true yokel. At length he managed to collect his thoughts, and said sneeringly—

"Now look here. Get out of this as fast as you can"

"Get out of this?" said Cardiff. "Of course we will. What the devil is there to tempt us to remain? We will go on to some place where the keepers do their work."

He stepped aside and walked on. I thought I could not do better than follow his example. We all three walked on. Cardiff was the smallest of us, and this interview was certainly a most remarkable instance of the triumph of mind over matter.

XII

A TRUE SPORTSMAN

ONE SUNDAY in winter I was out with Hyde, Cardiff, and Greenman in Surrey. Hyde persuaded us to go a couple of miles out of our usual course in order that he might visit an old poaching friend named Biggs, who was ill. We found him recovering, but very weak, and miserably poor. His illness had reduced him to destitution. He and his wife, both more than sixty years old, sat over a small fire of sticks. They assured us that for two months they had tasted nothing better than bread and weak tea without milk. The last bit of meat they had enjoyed was a rabbit which a labourer on a neighbouring farm had given them.

Hyde expressed regret that we had caught nothing that morning, but hoped that we might have better luck a little farther on, and promised to return with whatever was caught. A conversation ensued as to the best ground to try, and Biggs recommended that we should work a couple of fields within a hundred yards of a certain keeper's house. He assured us that hares always lay there, and that the conformation of the ground rendered it impossible for the keeper to see us by looking through his windows, which he could easily do if we traversed the fields farther away.

Contrary to our advice, he insisted on accompanying us, and

when we came near our destination volunteered to go a little way ahead and post himself in a position from which he could watch the keeper's house and give us warning if danger approached. We were soon on the fields, and in less than two minutes had put up a hare, and slipped a pair of greyhounds at him. Whilst that course was being run, another and much bigger and stronger hare bolted, and a second pair of dogs was slipped. The first course was a very short one, and, as often happens on coursing fields, the pair of dogs first slipped got on the second hare, which thus found itself pursued by four. All the dogs were good ones, and one—a grandson of the celebrated Misterton—was of quite extraordinary speed.

Then followed a course the like of which one sees only once or twice in a lifetime. The Misterton dog kept shooting past his rivals and compelling the hare to turn almost into their mouths, but the wily puss always managed to evade them. Time after time did they launch themselves at the cunning fugitive, but only to miss their aim and roll over and over on the ground. The hare must have turned some forty times, but always emerged unharmed from the cluster of dogs.

Before the course had been half run through we began to hear expressions of encouragement to the hare from the clump of bushes on the top of a high bank in which Biggs had placed himself. These were delivered in a tone of voice which was much too loud to be safe, considering the surroundings, and it looked as though the man who undertook to ward off danger was going to bring it down on us. As turn followed turn, and the hare balked his open-mouthed pursuers, the cries of delight, interlarded with oaths, rung clearer and clearer from the bushes. Presently the dogs, worn out with endless turning, began to grow weak, and gained but very little on the hare. Still, as the field was large, an occasional turn was taken.

At last the point was reached at which the hare began to draw away from the dogs. He made for a wood, and it was evident that if he reached it in safety the course was over. The excitement among us was so intense that not a whisper was dropped. The barrier was passed, and the dogs defeated. All eyes now turned instinctively to the clump from which the noises had proceeded. We turned just in time to see old Biggs fling his cap high into the air, give vent to three ringing cheers, and shout, "Bravo, hare! May you live forever!"

Strangely enough, the keeper did not hear the shouting, a circumstance which caused Hyde to remark, "He cannot be asleep; he must be mesmerized." We all joined in urging Biggs to go home. When we had got rid of him we again set to work, and the result was that when, an hour later, Hyde called at his house, he left enough stuff to keep the poor old fellow and his wife in provender for a fortnight.

XIII

TWO CONFESSIONS

THERE WAS A certain Justice of the Peace with whom I was very intimate. He was a large breeder of greyhounds, and was often in want of foster-mothers. I supplied him with several of these, and so won his friendship. He gave me free access to his stud dogs, and made me presents of whelps, and in various ways I became his debtor.

One morning I was unlucky enough to be identified by a couple of keepers, and, of course, was summoned. The case came before a bench of justices in a small town which I need not name, and my heart almost sank into my boots when I saw my friend the Colonel among the magistrates. The keepers swore that they saw me leave the road and set two dogs on to a hare, which was killed.

When asked what I had to say in defence, I replied that I was walking along the road, accompanied by two greyhounds, and seeing a hare on a field, could not resist the temptation to course it.

This statement was correct.

I noticed the magistrates conversing in an undertone for a few moments, and then the chairman announced that they considered the charge against me proved, and fined me twenty shillings.

I paid the money, and as this was the last case of the day I was getting out as quickly as possible when I saw the Colonel beckon me to him. He had come off the bench, and took me aside.

"I suppose, Colonel," said I, "you will never speak to me again?"

"Why not?" said he. "I don't believe that there is a man alive who keeps greyhounds but has done more or less poaching. I myself have done a little. I have never been able to resist the temptation to course a hare when I have put one up."

On another occasion I was fined rather smartly at Woolwich Police Court for poaching and assault. When I had paid the fine I was followed outside by an inspector of the Metropolitan Police, who holds that rank yet. He asked me quietly to walk round the corner as he wanted to speak to me, and then suggested an adjournment to a public house.

When we were inside he shook my hand warmly, and declared that he never missed the chance of making friends with a poacher. He assured me that when a mere youth, he had been fined repeatedly for poaching, and on one occasion suffered three months' imprisonment. He declared that he detested the Game Laws, and honoured everybody who broke them.

At first I felt inclined to doubt his statements. I thought he was trying to obtain information from me by throwing me off my guard, but further acquaintance showed that he spoke his mind. Indeed, it turned out that he came from the same district as Cardiff, and that the poaching feats of his early years were performed in the Welsh valleys.

XIV

TRAMPLED FLOWER-BEDS

ONE SUNDAY afternoon in summer Greenman, Hyde, Cardiff, Coke, and I were out in the country with the dogs. It was not the right time of year for poaching. The crops were so tall that it was impossible, except in a few places, to see a hare. We were simply taking a walk to exercise the dogs, and had a dozen of them with us.

About 6 P.M. we were approaching Addington, and as we passed the residence of Sir John Leonard lingered to admire his garden, which was then in full beauty. In front of the house stretches a lawn of a good many acres, and this was mown beautifully smooth. Scattered over it were flower-beds in all sorts of pleasing designs. The mould forming the beds was friable, and stood up some twelve inches above the level of the grass. Whilst we were discussing the merits of the flowers a hare ran across the road, just ahead of us, and dashed into the garden. The dogs swept after it like a troop of cavalry, breaking down the flowers, and throwing up the mould as they went. Soon the hare was turned, but, strangely enough, not caught. The dogs were too numerous, and were in one another's way.

When the hare emerged from the tangle the whole troop were again after her like a gust of wind, and the next turn saw a fresh area of flowers levelled, and further showers of mould scattered over the grass. Again and again did this happen. About a dozen turns were taken in all before poor puss was caught, and by then almost every bed on the lawn had been more or less injured.

Whilst the course was being run we heard voices shouting fiercely at the dogs, but we were too much excited to pay much attention to them. Presently, however, Sir John approached us, and furiously demanded our names and addresses. He was accompanied by another gentleman, who at first showed a disposition to lay hands on us, and assault the dogs. A shake or two brought him to his senses, and then the pair talked more calmly. Sir John began to bemoan his flowers, which he said had cost him a great deal, and could not be replaced that season. The ladies of his family, he declared, would be quite inconsolable.

At first we made no answer to his complaints, but seeing that he was deeply touched, I could not refrain from giving him an explanation of the occurrence. When he was in possession of the facts, he admitted that we were not to blame, but walked away, still lamenting his flowers.

XV

THE TABLES TURNED

W E WERE WALKING along a country road one fine September Sunday. Cardiff and Hyde were in front and I followed about eighty yards behind them with Greenman and Coke. Suddenly a hare ran across the road in front of them. The dogs dashed after it like bullets from a rifle, and it was caught before it had traversed more than two-thirds of the small field which it attempted to cross. I happened to be the first to scramble through the hedge, and, of course, ran towards the hare. Before I was halfway, however, a keeper burst through the opposite fence, and running with great agility reached the hare before me. The dogs were young ones and allowed him to take it from them.

When he had secured the hare he advanced towards me, brandishing a stick, and using fearful and wonderful language. I endeavoured to explain that we were walking along the road in a perfectly peaceable and law-abiding manner when the hare crossed, and the dogs naturally followed; but the more I explained the louder he swore. I then noticed that Cardiff, who, as I have said, was in front, had run at the same time as myself in a parallel direction, but on the farther side of a hedge, which prevented the keeper from seeing him. He was now through the hedge, and coming towards the scene of the altercation.

The keeper's back was turned towards him, and Cardiff, by a series of energetic gestures, indicated to me that I was to keep him in that position. The nearer Cardiff came the more hotly did I contradict the keeper, and kept his mind so occupied that Cardiff stole up behind him, snatched away the hare, which he was holding by the hind-legs, and hitting him across the face with it as he turned knocked him clean down. As he scrambled to his feet Cardiff thundered at him—"You blankety blank scoundrel, do you think I keep dogs to catch hares for you?"

I do not remember seeing such a sudden change come over anybody in the whole course of my life. The man gasped for breath, and was some minutes before he could use his voice. Cardiff advised him in a masterful tone to go home to his wife and children, as, if he interfered again with peaceable travellers, he might get into serious trouble. Whether he went home or not I do not know, but we saw him no more.

XVI

A ROMANCE OF THE FIELDS

RIVERHEAD was the only son of a widow, who was worth some £12,000. Before he was eighteen years old he was madly in love with a dairymaid who was in the service of his mother. The old lady saw how matters stood, and acted accordingly. She sent her son away from home, and in his absence talked plainly to the girl. She told her, quite truly, that the property was her own, and that she could dispose of it exactly as she pleased, and that if he married against her will she should leave every penny she possessed to her daughters, of whom she had three living.

Sarah was by no means easily persuaded to drop her lover. For a long time she clung to the belief that he would come like a thief in the night and bear her away. When, however, several months passed by, and not even a message had come from him, her faith waned, and she allowed herself to be persuaded to accept an outfit and free passage to New Zealand, and a gift of £50 in addition. Shortly afterwards Riverhead returned home, but found his lady-love flown, and after a few weeks gave up thinking about her.

It seems that courtships are short in New Zealand. At any rate, in less than a year after her arrival there Sarah was married to a comfortable farmer. In due course she became the mother of two children, a son and a daughter. Her husband took a great interest in cattle, and raised some valuable animals.

About four years after the marriage he purchased a young bull, at a high price, of which he was very proud. He was almost constantly inspecting him, and exhibiting him to neighbours and visitors. Getting up early one morning, as was his practice, he went for a walk in the fields. Breakfast time came and he did not return. Shortly afterwards search was made, and he was found dead, gored to death by his bull. The widow refused several offers of marriage, and although she kept on the farm for another five years, never afterwards became reconciled to her position, and ended by coming back to Kent and establishing a dairy for the supply of milk to the London market.

In the meantime Riverhead's mother had died, and her son had managed to get through her fortune. He did not squander it, but entered business as a speculative builder, and meeting with bad luck lost every penny.

He was living in London, and had not visited his native village for a long time. He knew nothing of the return of his old sweetheart, and none of us who were now his companions had ever heard of her existence. Matters were in this state when some half-dozen of us went for a night's outing. We took train to Bomstead in Surrey, and going in a zigzag way, passed Purley, and about eight o'clock the next morning found ourselves in the neighbourhood of Farleigh.

We chased hares at intervals, and at last were led by a course into the middle of a herd of milch cows. The hare was killed, and we were just turning away when we caught sight of a very well-dressed lady, portly and dignified, who was coming in our direction. She was followed by a country lassie and a boy some eight years old. It so happened that our respective paths brought our party and the lady within thirty yards of each other. All at once the stillness of the morning was broken by a shrill sound, approaching a shriek, from Riverhead, who cried, "Sarah." An instant's pause followed, and then came the response—

"My God, Sam, is that you?"

Too much moved for talking, he took her in his arms and imprinted on her lips, and face, and neck as many kisses as there are drops in a shower of rain. She wept, and the boy shrieked, and the maid looked frightened and bewildered. We, his comrades, were at first extremely puzzled, but the explanation came when the kissing was over. She insisted on having us in to breakfast, and whilst we indulged in copious draughts of new milk warm from the cows, Sam and Sarah billed and cooed like youngsters of sweet seventeen.

I am sorry to have to add that whilst Sarah was in New Zealand Sam had married, and was now a husband, and the father of four children. He could not, therefore, marry *her*. But all indications point to the conclusion that he would have done so if he could, and I may mention, in strict confidence, that that chance encounter, when the dewdrops glistened in the morning sunlight, was not the last occasion on which Sam and Sarah met.

XVII

TOM DAY

THERE IS PROBABLY no class of men more addicted to indulgence in intoxicating drinks than gamekeepers. The fact may be easily explained, and in some measure excused. Their long night-watches in the open air, and often in the coldest weather, prompt resort to stimulants which at least appear to keep up the animal heat of the body, and, at any rate, mitigate suffering by inducing partial insensibility.

The general life of the keeper is also conducive to this practice. When a man without education, and in most cases without ideas, is employed even during the daytime, in walking about in search of nothing in particular, he is much more apt to become a tippler than if he had some definite work to do; and the money with which the drink is purchased is easily obtained by selling some of his employer's game. On some estates rabbits are his recognised perquisite, and this is intended to deter him from appropriating more valuable property.

These drinking habits of keepers are well known to poachers, who occasionally turn them to good account. The old dodge of sending one or two of the gang to a public house to prime the keepers with liquor, whilst the others scour the woods, is not quite played out yet. Cardiff, who could sham drunkenness better than any actor I ever knew, invented a new variety of the trick. I have seen him shamble up to a keeper, with a couple of bottles of whisky sticking out of his pockets, induce the man to drink, and by pretending that he also was drinking gulp for gulp, reduce the fellow to helplessness.

One of the easiest of victims was an old man named Tom Day. He had to watch an estate of about three hundred acres, and he was quite unable to resist the attractions of whisky. We learned this by getting him to drink on the public road, where we first met, and soon we became bold enough to call at his house and present him with a bottle of whisky. Whenever we called in this way we were, of course, accompanied by dogs. Tom always brought us indoors, and kept us quiet for a half-hour or so, during which he consumed a considerable quantity of the spirit. Then he ascended a hill a few hundred yards away, and satisfied himself that nobody was in sight. After that he hastily fetched us outside, pointed out two or three fields on which he knew plenty of hares were to be found, and with many oaths informed us that he would, allow us fifteen minutes in which to work them, and that if we remained longer he would blow his whistle and alarm the district.

Of course this threat was mere bunkum, as fifteen minutes was ample time for our purpose. We nearly always caught enough to cover the cost of many bottles of whisky. As Tom grew older he became so fond of his couch that he gave very little attention to the game, but as his ground was surrounded by preserves which were very strictly watched, he always provided his employer with good sport when shooting time arrived.

Once a year Tom's employer permitted him to hold a private coursing meeting. To this farmers, shopkeepers, and others who had young greyhounds to try were invited. On such occasions a collection is made for the keeper, and, as a rule, few hares are killed. At one of these meetings Hyde and I joined the crowd to see the sport. It so happened that three or four hares in succession ran extremely well, and easily escaped from the young dogs. Finding the keeper a little apart from the others, Hyde remarked,

"Blowed if your hares don't run well, Tom." "So they ought, you rascal," was Tom's reply; "you keep them in practice."

On the last Boxing Day before Tom's death a few of us were making our way towards his cottage. We were traversing a footpath where there was a legal right of way, and were leading the dogs. This footpath ran through the property of the Right Honourable Joachim Goschen, Chancellor of the Exchequer. When we reached a certain point we came within hearing, and soon after within sight, of a party of gentlemen who were shooting rabbits. Two or three keepers angrily ordered us to turn back. We took no notice of their talk, and pushed on. One of the gentlemen shouted, "If you don't go back you'll probably get shot." Cardiff, who was in front, replied, "If you shoot me, my wife will send in a stiff bill to the Chancellor of the Exchequer." This made the company laugh, and they then explained that there was a small corner still unbeaten, which they wanted searched, and that after that was done we could come on with perfect safety.

Of course we waited until they had finished, and then passed on to Tom Day's ground. There we found several wounded hares, which had escaped from the shooting party, but which fell an easy prey to our dogs.

Poor old Tom! Many an exciting chase have we had over his fields and his furrows, and many a small bag has been turned into a large one by a few minutes' scamper over his refuge for the surrounding game. He is now gone to his long sleep, and the dewdrops which trickle through the matted grass roots above his head will affect him less than did the liquor of a different sort to which he was so partial when above ground.

XVIII

A TIMELY WARNING

IT WAS NINE O'CLOCK on a very cold night, and Hyde and I had been on foot since the morning. Towards nightfall we secured a good bag of fur and feathers, and were taking the precaution to avoid the roads, so that we did not touch a public house until we were within two miles of home. Then we had rather long drinks of hot whisky. After a half-hour's rest we walked another mile and found another public house, which we entered for the purpose of having a parting glass. To our surprise we found standing at the counter a man named Payne, head-keeper to a certain banker who maintains a large preserve. This good man was known in the neighbourhood as "Paney". A "cold night" was mutually exchanged by "Paney" and Hyde, and then we proceeded to sip our liquor. Hyde had his dog with him, and I had two. Ten minutes passed without a word being spoken, and the silence was becoming embarrassing to me. A certain restlessness in Hyde indicated that something was coming, or that the first drink was taking some effect. At length he spoke.

"Paney, they tell me you have taken to shooting dogs lately."

"Oh, they say a great many things about me which are not true."

"But, Paney, this tale must be true. Harry Jones's two dogs followed a hare into your wood, and both were shot. Bob White's bitch was shot at the same place, which is near the back of your house. And two dogs from Croydon were shot from among the laurels, almost as soon as they went through the hedge. No one saw the shooter, but you must know something about the matter."

"Well, suppose I do? What business had they there?"

"Paney, they may have had no right to be there; that I'll admit. But you had no right to shoot them. Now, I'll tell you why I mention the matter. Do you see this dog here?" (pointing to his own).

"Yes"

"Do you think you'll know him again?"

"I think I will."

"Well, Paney, I'll advise you to take a good look at him, so that you may know him again, for if you shoot this dog, I'll shoot you."

"You old perisher, I believe you would."

"You believe I would. Don't you *know* I would?"

"I believe you are bad enough for anything"

"Well, bad or good, I'll do what I promise. Whatever dogs you shoot, don't shoot mine!"

Another long silence, and a cold "good-night" ended the interview. Hyde's dog was not shot.

XIX

THE DEMON HARE

EVERY COURSING EXPERT is aware that there are some hares which no dog can catch, though they are few and far between. In the course of my life I have come across only three such. One was in King's County, Ireland, one in Wicklow, and one at Stainford-le-hope, Essex. All three excelled in speed, endurance, and cleverness in avoiding the dogs in turning, and strangely enough all three had peculiar white marks by which they could be recognised the moment they bolted. The first-named, which was probably the best of all, was called "White-hip" by the country people, because it bore on one hip a round white patch bigger than a crown piece. Dogs of renown were brought from far and near to course it, but it eluded them all. I have seen it run clean away from two cup winners after the first turn, and in a run of about a mile gain on them to the extent of two hundred yards. The subject of the present sketch was a hare of a different sort. It did not excel in speed, but in cleverness and endurance it was a marvel.

The run took place on Plumstead marshes, in the early morning. Two greyhounds were slipped at the hare. One was a very strong dog, about five years old, of great tenacity, a descendant of the celebrated Master Magrath. He was a terrific fighter, and worsted dozens of opponents, bulldogs among them. The other was a bitch, fast and clever, and about two years old. The first turn was taken very rapidly, and the second more quickly still. The course, in fact, looked like being an exceptionally easy one. Of the two dogs, the bitch was the faster, and put in some most excellent work. Turn followed turn, and still the hare was not caught. There was never a straight run of more than two hundred yards, and, as Greenman, Cardiff, and myself stood watching, the hare and dogs kept circling round us. When a dozen turns had been taken the bitch's strength began to fail, and she lagged somewhat. The dog, however, kept the sport going. Minute followed minute, and the relative strength of both dog and hare remained about the same. The straight runs were all through extremely short, and the whole course was run within an area of four acres. If we had known what was coming, we would have counted the turns, and I have been sorry ever since that we did not. I feel sure that they must have numbered nearly a hundred. The course lasted an almost incredible time, and the speed of the animals was at last reduced to a mere jog-trot. Still the fun was kept up. The beginning of the end was marked by the death of the bitch. She simply lay down and gave up the ghost. The tough old dog still stuck to his work, and took a multitude of turns after the loss of his mate. At last the run became quite laughable. Neither hare nor dog was able to run properly. They simply scrambled along, falling every few steps. We scarcely knew what to do with them, and simply looked on. The pace became slower and slower, until at last the dog lay down, and the hare, thinking doubtless that a rest had been fairly earned, lay down too, about three yards in front of him. We drew nearer the couple, and as we approached, the dog, game to the end, without getting on his legs tried to crawl on his belly towards the hare. When he had got within a yard, puss managed to stand up and stagger away about five yards. Both panted painfully, and the dog was quite too exhausted to kill the hare. We decided that the latter had fairly earned her life, and so we carried the dog some distance, and sat down to allow him to recover his breath. In about ten minutes we saw the hare, from where we sat, slowly creep away. She stopped to rest every few yards, but at length reached cover. The dog became so stiff that he was unable to walk, and had to be carried to the nearest railway station, and it was fully a fortnight before the stiffness left him. Several people prophesied that he would never run again, but he disappointed them all. When he recovered he ran just as well as before that long and memorable chase.

XX

BROTHERS AT LAST

ABOUT FOUR O'CLOCK one afternoon Mrs. Hyde heard a knock at her door, and on answering it found there a man whose leggings and velveteens proclaimed him a keeper. He inquired if Mr. Hyde was to be seen, and was told that he would be home in an hour. He promised to call later, and on being asked for his name gave it as Charley Chambers. Mrs. Hyde had often heard this name. In fact, it had appeared on some eight or ten summonses which her husband had received, as that of the prosecutor. She did not feel much concerned now, as she knew that her husband had not been in Chambers's neighbourhood for a considerable time, and yet his visit excited in her mind surprise and curiosity.

A couple of hours later Chambers called again, and this time was answered by Hyde, who asked him without any excessive politeness what he wanted. Chambers spoke softly as a cooing dove, and proposed that, as the beginning of his explanation, he should stand drinks at a neighbouring public house. Hyde eyed him with suspicion, and probably for the first time in his life hesitated as to what he should do. Chambers repeatedly assured him that he had a tale to tell, and at length curiosity overcame repugnance, and they adjourned to the tap-room indicated. A generous allowance of whisky having been placed on the table, Chambers unbosomed himself. He said that he had that morning received a month's notice to leave his situation, that he had been leading a fast life, and had therefore no money to fall back on, and that it was now absolutely necessary to raise the wind. He therefore proposed that Hyde should join him, and assist during the month in "working" the land which he was still supposed to guard.

It is evident that two men poaching in concert can secure much better results than they could apart. Besides, Chambers knew that Hyde possessed nets, snares, traps, and dogs; and, as there was no time to be lost, this was sufficient to account for his offer of co-operation. Hyde was won over, and resolving to begin business the very next day, he visited the landlord of a roadside public house a couple of miles from the boundary of Chamber's preserve. Farmers' carts laden with vegetables were constantly passing this point on their way to the London market, and Hyde arranged with the landlord that the game captured should be forwarded to an address in the neighbourhood of Leadenhall Market. The same evening he set his snares and traps, and with Chambers used drag nets to such effect that their spoil nearly filled two sacks. The following evening again saw them hard at work, with very similar result. Night after night the haul was repeated, without, however, making any appreciable difference in the quantity of game on the land. The fact is, Chambers's ground was quite surrounded by preserves of large extent, and, as every body acquainted with the matter knows, game cannot be confined to the land of its owner. Hares especially often travel long distances, and pass and repass certain points at least twice in the night and early morning.

The business went on gaily for over a week before Hyde mentioned the matter to any one. Then he dropped me a note, asking me to call on him. I did so, and learned how matters stood. The result was a descent by the whole gang on the area in question. A splendid night's sport rewarded our journey, but through fear of drawing attention to the place, and spoiling the efforts of our friend, we did not repeat the visit. It may be said with confidence that more game was captured on that preserve during that month than in any period of like duration. Towards the end the supply began to fall off, and doubtless Hyde did not exaggerate when he boasted that of the stock actually belonging to that land "there was not even a sparrow left".

Of course the "stuff" had to go at very low prices, but when accounts were all cleared up Hyde and Chambers had £38 each to take.

XXI

A RASH SHOT

O N A CERTAIN Sunday morning as Cardiff, Hyde, Coke, and I were crossing some fields, we happened to meet with two men, one of whom, named Yankers, carried a gun. The other walked very lame, and we did not even hear his name. We exchanged a few words with Yankers, whom we had met before, but his companion was quite silent.

We were going in the same general direction, and kept together for a short distance, when suddenly we found ourselves confronted by two keepers. One of these was elderly, and the other was much younger, and obviously new to his work. The old keeper indulged in some very tall talk, and expressed his determination to keep us in sight until he had procured assistance. Yankers, who had had some drink, answered him very sharply, and was, in fact, once or twice on the point of assaulting him. In the heat of the dispute he turned to his companion, the lame man, and ordered him to get away as quickly as he could. He had not gone very far before the old keeper realised that it was much easier to keep him in sight than any of the others, and so he told his young assistant to follow the lame man wherever he went, adding that he would look after us.

The assistant started in pursuit, but when he had gone about fifty yards Yankers yelled at him to stop. The young man halted and turned his face towards us, but was again ordered by his superior to proceed, on pain of instant dismissal. He walked on a few more paces, and was a second time brought to a standstill by a threat from Yankers, who this time informed him that if he advanced another inch he would shoot him.

For a few seconds he hesitated, and then, evidently fearing the loss of his job more than anything, he started off at a run. Suddenly the report of Yanker's gun caused all our hearts to sink, especially when it was answered by a shriek from the unfortunate keeper, who executed a step dance which was more remarkable for originality than grace. Luckily the gun was single-barrelled. Had it been double, there is not the slightest doubt that he would have shot the other keeper. As it was, he proceeded to reload as quickly as possible, but it was a muzzle-loader, and before it was charged Cardiff and Hyde intervened, calmed his rage somewhat, and extorted a promise from the old keeper that we should not be followed.

We then turned our attention to the wounded man, who by this time had walked back to us. He was rubbing down the backs of his thighs, as if in great pain, and muttering, "I'm shot! I'm shot!"

"You are all right, my boy," said Yankers; "I know I was too far away to do you much harm. When you go home you can get your mother to pick out the grains of shot with a pin. But let this be a warning to you; never interfere with poachers again."

Turning towards the old man, he said—

"As for you, you old perisher, I could shoot you as I would a rat! You are the one who ought to have had the dose. If you cross my path again and utter an uncivil word, you will know what to expect."

Yankers insisted on the keepers taking a different direction from that in which the lame man had gone. As for the rest of us, I need hardly say that we cleared out of that locality with all speed. Fearing that the telegraph wires might be brought into operation, we did not take the dogs home direct, but left them with a friendly farmer, and called for them a few days later.

In due course we received news of the injured man and his wounds, which were very slight, for he must have been almost seventy yards off when Yankers fired. The doctor picked a dozen pellets out of him, none of which lay more than skin deep. More frightened than hurt, he resigned his situation as gamekeeper, and became, as he had been before, a gardener's assistant.

This incident made us cautious. We recognised that we had had a very narrow escape from catastrophe, which, apart from the suffering it might have brought on us, we should ever have deplored. We poached for pleasure, and certainly would never dream of purchasing this at the cost of human life, or even of serious injury to any one. And so we thenceforth endeavoured to steer clear of desperate and unscrupulous characters of the Yankers type.

XXII

A ROUGH DUCKING

*"Yes, you may well defy me, you cowards, when you find
yourselves eight to one."*

THESE WORDS came from a tall, raw-boned keeper on a
March morning before sunrise, near Purley in Surrey.
There were eight of us, sure enough. We had been out all
night, and had regulated our movements so as to reach the spot at
which we had arrived—a place noted for hares—about daylight.
Almost the instant we left the high-road we got a chase, and within
five minutes we had several. Our enjoyment was rudely disturbed by the keeper in question, who rushed out of a wood, and
made for the nearest of the party as if bent upon arresting him.
When, however, he saw how many he had to deal with he halted
and began blowing his whistle vigorously. He was quickly surrounded and ordered to cease blowing, with the alternative of
having the whistle knocked out of his mouth. Finding himself
outnumbered, he submitted with all the grace he could command. Three stood guard over him, whilst the other five coursed
hares before, behind, and around him. In a very short time the
dogs were exhausted, and having strongly advised him to remain
where he was, and make no noise for at least fifteen minutes, we
began to move off. It was at this stage, and when we had gone a
few steps away, that he indulged in the retort—

"Yes, you may well defy me, you cowards, when you find yourselves eight to one."

In seven of the eight this remark excited nothing but merri-
ment. We old hands never forgot that "hard words break no
bones" and as long as we secured plenty of sport we were quite
content to leave our opponents a preponderance or even a monop-
oly of bad language. And so seven of the eight of us laughed
heartily. There was, however, one among us who only occasionally accompanied the gang, and who greatly prided himself on his
ability as a boxer. His name was Barwick. He now announced that
he was not accustomed to hearing himself described as a coward,
and that he did not feel inclined to submit quietly to the insult.
Notwithstanding our remonstrances, he challenged the keeper to
single combat. The latter could not have had such a very bad opinion of us, notwithstanding his remark, for he at once agreed to
pick up the glove, provided the remainder of us promised to stand
by and show fairplay. Seeing that the men were determined to
fight, we gave the necessary promise, and hostilities commenced,
and the set-to took place on a perfectly level sward, about twenty
yards from the brink of a small lake.

Although Barwick was stoutly built, he was much the smaller
man of the two. In the early stages of the conflict, however, his
knowledge of the science of boxing gave him a distinct advantage
over his opponent. He planted at least two blows for the other fellow's one. But Barwick was not in condition. He was much too
fat, whilst the keeper, although muscular, was as lean as a greyhound, and he planted some very heavy blows, until at length it
became painfully obvious that Barwick's wind was failing. He
stuck to his task doggedly through a couple of rounds in which
his exhaustion was very noticeable, and I, for one, began to fear
that he would have to acknowledge defeat.

The swaying of the fighters brought them ever nearer the
border of the lake, and when matters appeared to be drawing
towards an end, Barwick, in a moment of fury, seized his opponent round the waist, ran to the over-hanging bank, and jumped

clean into the water. The depth was not great—probably not over five feet near the edge. Both men, of, course, went under, but immediately on rising Barwick, who was a swimmer, scrambled towards a spot where the bank was low, and was hauled on to dry ground. The keeper, on the other hand, was no swimmer, and although appearing to touch bottom with his feet, he became dazed, floundered about, and instead of coming towards the bank stumbled into deeper water. In a few seconds it became obvious to all of us that, if left to himself, the man would drown.

Our party contained several swimmers, but the morning was shockingly cold, we were more than twenty miles distant from home, and under such circumstances water feels disagreeably wet. Barwick, who was already wet, was appealed to by all to re-enter the water, but by this time he was in a pitiable condition. His teeth were chattering with cold, his breath was short, and his strength was almost gone. Half persuaded, half forced, he, however, again entered, and being lucky enough to grasp the man's clothing almost immediately, he hauled him to the brink without difficulty. The unfortunate keeper was indeed very nearly drowned. After being drawn out on the grass, he was gasping some time before he could stand. The majority of the party hurried Barwick off at a run in order to keep up his circulation, but two of us remained behind in order to see the keeper out of danger. In a short time he was able to speak, and treated us to the choicest collection of oaths it has ever been my privilege to hear. We left him still blaspheming.

When we caught Barwick up we found him stripped naked, and being rubbed dry by our friends. He could not, of course, don his wet clothes, and so we had to furnish him from among us with a makeshift suit. No one was willing to hand over his trousers, but the absence of that garment was to some extent hidden by a very long overcoat which Greenman contributed. When we had placed three or four miles between us and the scene of conflict, we entered a cottage and persuaded the good man to sell us an old pair of trousers.

XXIII

A NOVEL POINT

THE DAY WAS Sunday, the month was August, and the weather was extremely warm. We—Greenman, Cardiff, and I—after some months' absence, had run down to see Hyde. Much of the corn was cut, and we thought it time to arrange for a night out with the dogs. After walking some miles, we had just refreshed ourselves at a wayside inn, and were resting on the grass of Banstead Common, Surrey. Hyde was not in a talkative mood, but nevertheless he made clear to us that as some crops were still standing, and the leaves were yet on the bushes and trees, it was too early to use greyhounds. For a considerable time he lay very quiet, and appeared to be asleep. At length he started up and said—

"Chaps, can any of you borrow a setter or a pointer? Any old one, lame or lazy, will do. I have had an idea in my head for a long time, and if you can borrow the dog I want I'll promise you the biggest night's haul we have ever yet made."

We talked the matter over. Setters and pointers were scarce in London. Cardiff knew of none; I knew of none; but fortunately Greenman could tell us of one, a pointer. It had been the property of a nobleman, but was now old, and was kept as a pet by the landlord of a public house somewhere in the neighbourhood of Denmark Hill. Greenman said he felt sure he could borrow it, as he was on very friendly terms with its owner. This settled, Hyde declared that if we wanted him to keep his promise of making a good bag, we must bring down the dog before the 1st of September.

As we discussed the exact date of our coming, Hyde insisted, much to my bewilderment, that a bright night would not suit his purpose; and finally, after calculating the times of rising and setting of the moon for a fortnight in advance, it was agreed that we would come down on the last Saturday night of August.

My own experience of setters and pointers began with babyhood, and in the course of a fairly long life I had never known them to be used for other than one purpose. They were invariably shot over. When those dogs scent game they "set" or "point" which, in plain language, means that they stand still until the sportsman behind them steps forward with his gun, flushes or bolts the game, and shoots at it. From the moment, therefore, that Hyde spoke of setters or pointers my thoughts ran on shooting. He puzzled me exceedingly by saying that a bright night would not suit, but I still never doubted that shooting was intended. When all the details were arranged, I remarked—

"I suppose, Hyde, we shall bring down the guns?"

"Indeed," he replied, "you shall do nothing of the sort. What in thunder is the good of bringing guns to a place like this! Before you fired your sixth shot you would have a small mob of people round you. Leave your guns at home, but if you bring along some bags, about the size of large pillowcases, you'll probably find them useful."

This oracular remark left us more puzzled than before. We all three plied him with questions as to his programme for the night, and wanted to know what on earth was the good of bringing down a pointer if he did not mean to shoot. For replies we got smiles, and later on hearty laughter, but no enlightenment. Hyde had evidently made up his mind to give us a surprise.

The last Saturday of August arrived in due course. The weather was dry and the sky but slightly clouded. The moon set about

11 P.M., and up to that hour the night was bright. We reached Hyde's cottage with our fat old pointer about 10.30. A more use-less-looking animal for poaching purposes could hardly be imagined. Poachers are often betrayed into the hands of their enemies by their dogs, but with this one I would undertake to pass scores of gamekeepers without exciting the slightest suspicion.

Hyde questioned Greenman closely as to whether the dog had ever actually worked under a gun, and on being assured that he had, expressed himself thoroughly satisfied. He next told us that we should sally out about 12 o'clock, by which time, he hoped, the keepers would have gone home.

When the time came for starting Hyde brought forth from an inner room what is known as a dragnet, which may as well be described. It was about forty yards in length, twenty feet in width, and had meshes about an inch square. It was composed of such fine material that notwithstanding its size it easily fitted into the "hare pocket" of Hyde's jacket. The only other implement with which he armed himself was a small lantern of the toy variety, very light, and made to hold stumps of candle. Hundreds of the same pattern may be seen in the suburbs any warm night, in the hands of children. Throwing a bag over his shoulder, he invited us to set forward.

We kept to the high-road for about a mile, and then, crossing a wooden fence, found ourselves in a grass field. Silently we marched until we reached an extensive hollow where the ground had been cropped and was now stubble. Hyde produced the lantern, and getting us all to stand close round him so as to hide the flame, struck a match and lighted his candle. By means of a collar, which he had ready, he hung the lantern from the dog's neck. I now noticed that a pasteboard arrangement inside the glass permitted very little light to escape; mere pin-points showed themselves at the front and at either side. The net was next unfolded, and Cardiff and I were directed to work it.

The way in which dragnets are usually worked is as follows:—
the net is drawn out to its full length, and two men take each a

corner. Walking as far apart as possible, they keep the front of the net shoulder high, while the back, which is generally weighted, trails the ground. In this manner they walk abreast across a field, and if they happen to come upon a covey of partridges, the moment the birds make their presence known the net is dropped.

This is the old plan, but it has drawbacks. Wherever game is preserved bushes are allowed to grow at intervals over the fields. Many of these cannot be seen at night. The result is that the net often gets entangled and torn, and is sometimes rendered useless. In any case a great deal of time is wasted in shaking it free. In stubble land bushes are stuck in the ground by the keepers for this purpose. Every foot of the ground has to be traversed in order to make sure that no birds are left behind. Hyde's plan was a great improvement on the foregoing. When all was ready he gave his orders.

"Now, chaps, listen. You two with the net, keep your eyes open. When you see *the light point* keep thirty yards to the right, get in front of it, and drag the net towards the lantern. The birds are sure to be within a few feet of the dog's nose, and will lie close. Most likely they won't rise at all. If they do rise, of course you drop the net at once. If they don't, you drag it gently forward until it is well over the dog, then drop it, and they are ours."

"You, Greenman, follow the dog up, and encourage him to work. He knows you best. I will pick up the birds. I know best how to do it. Now march straight ahead."

We moved on. The old dog was so long out of practice that at first he appeared to be ignorant of his business. Probably his previous owner, the nobleman already mentioned, had never worked him at night. For a couple of minutes he clung to Greenman's knees, but then he began to understand what was wanted of him. Before we had proceeded a hundred yards he got a scent and *the light pointed*. Swiftly and noiselessly Cardiff and I described a semicircle to the front and spread out our net. We drew it forward softly, keeping it well off the ground, and when it was just over lantern and dog dropped it, and held it down.

Up to the moment of dropping it I had serious doubts as to whether there were any birds beneath, but my mind was quickly set at rest on that point. Such a bounding and fluttering I had never witnessed before. Instantly Hyde was down on them like a terrier on rats. By a dexterous twist of the neck they were, one after another, reduced to silence, and in less than a minute the net was removed and Hyde counted eight partridges into his bag. Greenman, Cardiff, and I were delighted, but Hyde was rather disappointed, and declared that, the year being a splendid one for partridges, he had not thought that there could be such a small covey on the estate.

With a note of triumph in his merry voice Greenman again urged the dog forward. Something like two hundred yards were covered, and again *the light pointed*. This time we bagged eleven. We had not moved more than forty yards when a third point took place, but the birds were probably awakened by the second capture, and flew before they were properly covered by the net. This throw brought us only four. After that luck came fast and furious. We soon lost count of our birds, and Hyde had to call on Greenman to carry some of them.

Two or three times some one or other of the party thought he heard a noise, which might mean danger. On each of those occasions Hyde promptly blew out the light, and insisted on moving away a considerable distance. We met, however, with no interference, and continued our pointing, and dragging, and bagging until we were quite tired. It was hard to coax Hyde away from the ground. He protested that there was a considerable area still untouched, and implored us to come again the following night, so as to make a clean job of it. We, however, had our ordinary work to attend to on the Monday, and did not feel equal to the task of remaining out of bed on two successive nights.

We reached Hyde's cottage shortly before daybreak, made a large fire, partook of a hearty breakfast, and counted the birds. They numbered two hundred and fourteen! For the twentieth time at least we acknowledged in all possible sincerity that Hyde deserved his title of "King of the Poachers".

Hyde insisted on an equal division of the spoil. This, however, was found impracticable. Some of us, neglecting his advice, had come unprovided with bags. We all three, nevertheless, carried away more than we wanted. For my own part, I made presents of game to most of my friends, and during the fortnight following that night on the stubble I ate partridge morning, noon, and night.

XXIV

TIPSY PHEASANTS

GREENMAN, ALTHOUGH a very good fellow, had one weakness which he could not quite overcome. He was brought up in a part of the country where cock-fighting was practised, and acquired such a liking for it at an early age that he could never afterwards be brought to admit that it had any objectionable features. Many a time did we try to persuade him that it was cruel, cowardly, objectless, and degrading. He would have none of our logic, and maintained with the utmost firmness, that it was an exhilarating form of sport, and that his only objection to London was that cock-fighting could not be enjoyed there.

One morning the old subject was under discussion. We had walked about seven miles in order to get some coursing, and now sat on a heap of stones, waiting for day to break. Cardiff was maintaining the humane view, and Greenman was contending that although coursing was good enough in its way, it could not be compared with cock-fighting.

At length Hyde broke in, and asked Greenman why, if he liked to see birds fight, he did not make pheasants fight instead of poultry, especially as he could wring their necks when they fell exhausted. This remark interested all of us, and we inquired rather eagerly whether pheasants could be induced to fight. Hyde replied that there was no difficulty about the matter. All that was needed was to make them drunk, and if we provided him with a quart of whisky or rum, he would undertake to show Greenman all the fighting he wanted, and procure us some pheasants as well.

The whisky was provided in due course, and by the following Saturday night Hyde had everything ready. He procured about two quarts of barley, which he steeped in water for two or three days until the grains were swollen. On Friday evening he strained off the water and poured the whisky over the barley, when the alcohol of the whisky expelled the water from the grain and took its place.

On Saturday night, taking the barley out with us in a small canvas bag, we chased rabbits and hares in the moonlight, and arranged our movements so that we reached a certain wood about daybreak, which was surrounded by a boarded fence and well stocked with pheasants. Hyde now took possession of the barley, and having placed us among some bushes where we could not be seen very readily, proceeded to arrange for the combat.

He selected a spot about thirty yards from the wood, where the ground was bare of grass, and placed there in a little heap a couple of handfuls of barley. From this to the wood he shook a thin line of the grain, and just outside the fence scattered more widely a small handful. Some twenty yards farther down he repeated the operation, and again in a third place. Having exhausted his stock of barley, he took his stand with the rest of us in the clump of bushes.

We had to wait a considerable time before any pheasants appeared; but, when they did come, they came quickly. The first one that struck the train of barley pecked energetically for a minute or so, and then uttered a peculiar sound, which, I suppose, was a call to his mate. This was repeated several times, and soon brought half-a-dozen others to the spot. They pecked and pecked as if to save their lives, and ran along the train as if eager to forestall one another. Presently the little heap of grain was reached.

By this time they had become rather noisy, and soon several others gained the flock. In about ten minutes from the first discovery of the barley the fighting began, and stiff fighting it was, without doubt. Hyde had been telling us that pheasants were quite as pugnacious, and possessed as much endurance, as game-cocks, and the combat we witnessed seemed to prove the truth of his statements. The most curious part of the business was that the hens fought just as well as the cocks. They did not single out opponents as sober poultry do, but just fell to and fought every-thing they met. They soon got in a tangle, and each bird was fight-ing all the others in a general way. I fancy that if all the members of the Royal Humane Society and the Humanitarian League had been there, not one of them could have refrained from laughing.

At last the pace began to tell. There was no flinching. Not a single bird ran. One by one, however, they fell exhausted, and lay gasping for breath. Sometimes, after a short rest, a strong one would scramble on his legs, and fight another round, but in a few minutes more they were all quite used up. Two of our party then ran down and secured eight birds. Presently another fight began round the second heap of grain, but when during its progress we observed two keepers some distance away, we thought it prudent to move, as we were well known thereabouts; so we ended that fight rather prematurely, but nevertheless secured five more birds.

Greenman declared that it was the best fight he had witnessed for twenty years. Cardiff vowed that it was the most rascally method of catching pheasants that had ever been invented. We all agreed that it was a pity that a representative of the Independent Order of Good Templars, or some teetotal advocate, was not present, as the combat would have provided him with an unan-swerable argument against the use of intoxicating drinks. Anyhow, we repeated the trick on a good many subsequent occa-sions, and always netted a fair number of pheasants.

I may mention here that the same plan may be applied to par-tridges. They are almost as pugnacious as pheasants. If a few handfuls of straw are placed in a grass field in a position where it can be seen it will attract partridges, and if grain, prepared in the way I have described, is strewn around it, the birds may be caught quite readily. It really does not matter whether they fight or not; if they get sufficiently intoxicated they become quite helpless. I have caught plover and seagull in this way. One gull whose wings I clipped remained in my possession as a pet for more than nine years, and in the end died of old age.

XXV

POACHING BY STEAMBOAT

I F HE WOULD ensure continued success, a poacher must be prepared to assume as many different disguises as possible. Two or three members of our party were men of remarkable appearance, and when they, or any of them, were absent, others dressed so as to resemble them. Greenman, for instance, was very tall, and had jet-black whiskers, and he wore a hat of uncommon shape. Another of the party was equally tall, and when Greenman remained at home this man often wore a hat of the sort alluded to, and when he got out in the country drew from his pocket a pair of ample black whiskers which made him bear a striking resemblance to his mate. Once, at least, this saved him from a heavy fine.

We also varied our method of approaching a preserve in every way open to us. Sometimes we went into the country by brake, sometimes in two or three dog-carts, which traversed different roads and met at a spot previously agreed on, and sometimes by train, when we seldom alighted twice within two months at the same station. But a time came when we found it desirable to make a new departure, and this was nothing less than chartering a steamboat to take us to the marshes which lay forty or fifty miles away, at the mouth of the Thames.

Cardiff was an engineer, and was, of course, acquainted with many of the men in his trade in the east and south of London. There is a certain dock, which need not be named here, in which gentlemen's yachts lie up during the winter months. These are looked after by caretakers, and in the case of steam-yachts the caretaker is generally an engineer, whose duty is to keep the vessel clean and the machinery in working order. To make sure of this it is sometimes necessary to put the yacht in motion, and therefore it is not unusual for the man to take her out of the dock and into the open river at high tide, of course with the aid of an assistant.

Cardiff approached one of those men, and struck a bargain with him. The use of the yacht was secured from Saturday to Sunday night or Monday morning for £2, 10s. The vessel was a small one, but large enough to accommodate fifteen of us, and so the charge to each was small. We selected a Saturday on which the tide was at its height about 10 P.M. The yachtsman had come out by the morning tide, and dropping down the river, he lay at a convenient spot where during the day two of our men got nearly twenty dogs aboard. About high tide we slid aboard in twos and threes, and by three o'clock next morning found ourselves lying off Southminster marshes, which face the German Ocean. We soon found a suitable spot for disembarking, and having got ashore, spread ourselves over the marshes.

I may mention that the Southminster marshes are noted for the number of their hares. Regular coursing matches take place there every winter, but it is generally found necessary to shoot a number of hares before coursing is attempted, for when hares are too plentiful a great many trials are spoiled. A pair of dogs may be slipped at a hare, and when they have run a considerable distance a second hare may bolt under their noses. Sometimes the dogs will separate, one following each hare; or sometimes both dogs will follow the fresh quarry. If they have already had a tough spin, the second hare sometimes runs them almost to a standstill, so that they run at a great disadvantage in subsequent trials. Our first descent on these marshes took place in the month of August. Neither coursing nor shooting had begun that season, and we found the place literally full of hares. The season had been an exceptionally favourable one for their breeding, and they lay probably twenty to the acre.

In a few minutes the work of slaughter commenced. At first we slipped the dogs in pairs, orthodox fashion, but very soon found that that plan did not answer. Whilst we were watching the first course half-a-dozen hares escaped, and before the dogs which had just run could be caught they were on to a fresh hare. A second pair was slipped, and then a third, and before many minutes had elapsed the whole pack was loose. We tried to secure some measure of fair play by scattering as much as possible. The dogs, generally speaking, kept near their masters, and every few yards we walked we found a hare, many of them being caught before they got on their legs. Some, however, showed magnificent sport, and in half-an-hour nearly all the dogs were exhausted, when we picked them up, as best we could, intending to give them a rest.

Whilst a few of us were standing together we noticed Coke, some four hundred yards away, standing over a dog with his hands in his trousers' pockets, and evidently in a state of deep contemplation. At this time Coke had a bitch about fourteen months old which he valued very highly, and which he expected to win, several stakes. All Coke's young dogs were invariably expected to win fabulous sums, but somehow or other mishaps occurred, and very little was actually won. This time, however, his hopes were shared by all of us, for the greyhound in question was certainly of exceptional quality. When I saw him thus standing over her I concluded that she had hurt herself, and walked towards him to see what was wrong. As I approached I noticed that she lay flat on the ground, on her side, with her limbs extended. "Has she broken her leg?" I asked, and Coke replied in a tone of deep melancholy, "No, she has broken her heart." She had indeed run herself to a complete standstill. Five dead hares, caught single-handed, showed how busy she had been, getting on to fresh hare after fresh hare, until at last she could run no further. There she lay at last, and threats and caresses were alike powerless to move her.

We lifted her up and set her on her legs, but the moment we took our hands off she dropped down like a lump of wood; her limbs were as stiff as if she had been dead a week. Coke loudly bewailed his hard fate, and reproached himself with his folly in bringing her there at all. At length he took her up in his arms and carried her to the yacht. She recovered, but never won a shilling, although she turned out a very good poacher.

After half-an-hour's rest we again loosed the animals. Hare after hare fell until it was obvious that the dogs were completely used up. There was, however, one exception, my Nellie. In another part of this volume her breeding is described. On this occasion, during the early part of the business, she was passed by the thoroughbreds again and again. Dozens of times did this happen. But the longer the running lasted the more did her strength tell, and at last she made us all laugh by passing by the fastest dogs on the field. This was the first, but not by any means the last time that she performed this feat, and no one could notice the slightest difference in her speed from start to finish. At last even Nellie was placed on the lead, and dogs, hares, and men returned aboard the yacht. When we counted our hares we found that they numbered seventy-two.

As it was still early morning we steamed northward along the Essex coast, marked suitable places for disembarking on future trips, and enjoyed what turned out to be a very fine day. Towards evening we got the dogs ashore not a thousand miles from Greenwich, and when the shades of night descended managed to discharge our cargo of hares, and divide them as fairly as possible. By next morning the yacht was safe and secure in her old moorings. The last word of the skipper, who in addition to his £2, 10s. received four hares, was that he hoped we'd soon repeat the voyage.

During our stay on the marshes we met with no disturbance. The country around there is somewhat thinly populated, and keepers are few and far between. Herdsmen live on the marshes, but generally at distances of two or three miles apart, and so they could never constitute a menace to a party such as ours. If poach-

ers approached the marshes from the land side they might be followed, but they are not expected to come from the sea, and the
coast-line is much too extensive to defend. We often visited
Southminster afterwards, and occasionally a shepherd would
make his appearance and treat us to a volley of curses. We generally silenced him by presenting him with a pouch of tobacco and
a long drink of whisky.

When time did not permit us to go as far as Southminster we
were obliged to land at a point nearer home, and where the
ground was more closely watched. We have landed more than
once at Cliffe, where regular coursing meetings were held, which
we frequently attended. There we encountered two or more
keepers, to whom some of us were known. These kept in the
background, or tied pocket-handkerchiefs over their faces, whilst
the fellows who were not known inspired the enemy with a
wholesome caution. During our visits to the regular coursing
meetings there, Cardiff took a keen delight in inquiring of the
keepers whether they were much annoyed by poachers. They
generally declared that they were, and told tales of encounter, all
going to show that each keeper could thrash at least five poachers. Knowing what we did about the actual facts, we found these
stories very diverting.

On one occasion, during the pause for lunch, a young keeper
told a very smart tale of an encounter with three poachers. When
he caught them up he collared one, and drawing some cord from
his pocket, tied his arms and legs in such a way as prevented him
from either moving or releasing himself. The second he tied in a
somewhat similar manner to a gate-post, and the third he
marched before him to the nearest house, where he obtained
assistance and returned for the others. Of course we applauded
his prowess. It happened that about three months afterwards we
met this very keeper on the same Cliffe marshes. He tried a little
bluster, but soon changed his tune, and blew with remarkable
vigour a loud-sounding whistle. Cardiff, who had a handkerchief
over his face, approached him, and drawing forth some cord and

dog leads, informed him that if he blew another blast he would tie him hand and foot, and leave him on the ground for the crows to pick his eyes out. The blowing ceased immediately.

Poaching by steamboat we found extremely interesting, safe, and profitable. When we met with serious interruption, as we did once or twice, we only needed to re-embark, steam on two or three miles, and make a fresh descent. This method threw open to us a much larger area than we could otherwise approach, and dogs and men reached the ground fresh. The high embankment which runs along the Thames, down from Woolwich, screened our little vessel from the observation of those on land, and a small gangway which we always carried enabled us to land easily.

We did not always use the same yacht, but during the first three or four seasons we made no change, using one which was the property of a Scottish colonel who, I have since learned, is one of the strictest game preservers in Scotland. He little knew the use to which, in his absence, his boat was put. If he should read these pages, let him draw consolation from the fact that he has unconsciously assisted in filling many an empty stomach. In some of our steamboat expeditions we captured more hares than we knew what to do with, and a spare one, judiciously bestowed, always imparted joy to a poor family in a London slum.

XXVI

A FRIEND IN COURT

On the 4th of August 189– I and Riverhead were each fined, at Croydon Town Hall, £1 and 13s. 6d. costs for killing hares on the land of Mr. Gladstone at Addinton, in Surrey. Five months later I was again summoned, this time to the Old Bailey, to act as juryman. From the dock to the jury-box might seem an upward step, but it was one which at the moment I did not desire to take. I knew that attending the Old Bailey meant being absent a week or more from my work, and that was a luxury which I could ill afford. I did all I could to be excused from serving, but the judge was inexorable. Circumstances which occurred afterwards made me feel glad that I had been compelled to remain.

Almost immediately I was sworn as one of a jury which proceeded to try cases before the Common Sergeant, Sir Forrest Fulton. During the first three days the prisoners who were brought before us were of the sort a countryman of mine has described as "black-guard criminals". Pickpockets, shoplifters, coiners, and a modern highwayman who robbed with violence not only men, but women, excited no compassion in our breasts.

At length, however, a case of a different character arose. Two men of the labouring class were placed in the dock and charged with night-poaching and assaulting gamekeepers with bludgeons. Both bore marks of recent wounds, and those of one must have been terribly severe, and were not yet half healed. In reference to this man a gentleman wrote a letter to the *Star*, in which the following passage occurs:—

"I was present soon after the wretched poacher was captured at Worcester Park, and was horror-stricken with the brutality that had been used by about a dozen well-armed men in the capture. When I found that the poacher was dazed and bleeding I ventured to remonstrate with the keepers and their leader, the occupier of the land, who is a brother-in-law to the landlord, and very nearly got my head broken for my pains. I deeply regret not having been able to attend the Old Bailey to speak for the unhappy man."

This was written after the trial.

The Old Bailey method of summoning jurors is to summon for each session the total number required from one London parish. Every parish is taken in turn, and it takes about two years to get over the whole of London in this way. It follows from this that many of the jurors on each panel are personally acquainted with one another. On the jury on which I sat there were five men whom I knew, and two of these were personal friends. This will, perhaps, help to explain what follows.

The prisoners were not defended by counsel, and seemed incapable of saying a word for themselves. The prosecuting counsel made out a very strong case against them. Two keepers were produced who had sustained very bad injuries indeed, and a bludgeon was held up for the jury to inspect, which it was represented one of the poachers had carried for purposes of offence in case of interruption.

In looking at the bludgeon I noticed that it had on one end a brass fitting, and closer inspection showed it to be nothing more or less than the first section of the long handle of a chimney-sweep's broom. A few questions put to the police witnesses elicited an acknowledgment of this fact.

I then explained to the court that poachers often used sweeps' brooms, not as weapons of offence, but as implements of their trade. Their plan was to place the purse-nets over the mouths of the rabbit-holes, push the brooms or, at any rate, the handle, into one of the holes and rattle it about. By this means the rabbits were induced to bolt, and were caught in the nets. This reduced the crime very considerably. According to law the poacher is not liable to the heavier punishment unless he carries the bludgeon for purposes of offence. The judge seemed to reflect for a moment, and acknowledged the importance of the point made, but in all other respects charged strongly against the prisoners. Then he placed the case in the hand of the jury.

Long experience in another department of human affairs had taught me the hypnotic influence over men of a first and emphatic expression of opinion. I sat in the front seat of the jury-box, and standing up I faced my colleagues and said, with all the energy I could command:—

"Gentlemen, I'll never convict these men. For any crime which they may have committed they have been punished far too harshly already. Whatever you may say or do, my verdict is decided on."

I am afraid I must have spoken more loudly than I intended, for a very audible titter came from different parts of the chamber. One of my friends immediately declared that he hated the Game Laws, and did not like to be made an instrument of in giving effect to them. Others nodded assent, and for a moment I thought we were going to agree without leaving the box, as we had done in all previous cases.

In that hope, however, I was disappointed. One man declared emphatically his intention of holding out for a conviction, and others appeared doubtful. After some minutes spent in discussing the evidence, the judge remarked that we had better retire and consider the matter in a more leisurely way. We did as he desired. Locked in the jury room we thrashed the case out for a good half-hour, and as we had not come to an agreement somebody suggested that a vote be taken with a view to finding out how we stood. Ten hands were held up for an acquittal and two for a conviction. Then an elderly gentleman raised his voice, who had said very little during the discussion. He delivered himself somewhat as follows:—

"Gentlemen, I have been sitting on juries for nearly forty years, and would like to make one or two remarks which are prompted by experience. In the first place, I would say that the notion that the verdict of a jury is arrived at unanimously is in very many cases erroneous. It is more frequently the verdict of the majority. The minority recognise that disagreement would involve expense and trouble, and therefore wisely give way.

"The vote just taken shows a nearer approach to unanimity than is generally obtainable. I would ask you two gentlemen who are in opposition whether it is wise to be obstinate in this case. Remember that you are not on the side of mercy."

This appeal had an immediate effect. The two recalcitrant jurors gave way. The foreman seemed the weariest of the twelve, and I took care to walk immediately behind him as we marched in single file back into the court. An official muttered the legal formula ending with "Guilty or not guilty?" The foreman whispered almost inaudibly, "Not guilty." The official added, "Not guilty on all the counts?" The foreman was silent. I blurted over his shoulder, "Not guilty on all the counts," a phrase which the foreman repeated.

"Gentlemen," said the judge, "I dispense with your services."

We were not, however, allowed to go, but, whether as a punishment or not, were compelled to hang about the court until the end of the session.

A barrister who had noticed the active part I took in the case followed me out and said—

"I would like you to tell me your opinion of the case you have just tried."

"I think," I replied, "that our opinion may be gathered from the verdict."

"Just so," said he, "but I would like to understand the process of reasoning by which, you arrived at that verdict."

"The fact is," said I, "some of us are poachers ourselves."

He answered "I thought so; but you have done a good day's work. The case was very like a malicious prosecution."

I did not need a barrister to tell me of good work I had accomplished; nevertheless I was glad to know that at least one member of the legal profession was of the same turn of mind as myself.

XXVII

NELLIE

I N HIS WELL-KNOWN work, "The Gamekeeper at Home" Richard Jefferies quotes the gamekeeper as saying of his dogs: "I never makes 'em learn no tricks, because I don't like to see 'em made fools of." He adds, "I have observed that almost all those whose labour lies in the fields, and who go down to their business in the green meadows, admit the animal world to a share in the faculty of reason."

There are, of course, many animals to whom it would be folly to attribute the power of thinking (and, unfortunately, a not inconsiderable number of human beings as well), but that some animals can reason with startling correctness no one who has known my Nellie can for a moment doubt. Several times in the course of her career I have had to make her "board out". She was never absent from our expeditions, and when a scuffle occurred she always took a leading part in it. Hence the necessity for placing her out of sight occasionally to avoid identification. It is a remarkable fact that three different men with whom I thus placed her commented on her in exactly similar terms when I removed her. Their words were, "She is almost human."

The statement is widely accepted that the poacher's dog is always like his master, and that, in short, his character reflects his training. But my Nellie has frequently done things to which, from the very nature of the case, she could not be trained, and which were the very opposite of what her instinct prompted. On numberless occasions when a hare has bolted it has run in a certain direction, but Nellie, who knew the ground, was well aware that it could not escape that way, and instead of following it as her instinct would prompt, she shot off to the right or the left, to a gap or a gate through which she knew it must pass. Was it instinct that prompted her? Was it not the soundest exercise of reason? Some of her performances were even more remarkable. We often had young thoroughbred greyhounds in our pack, which, though extremely fast, were very bad catchers. At an early stage of her career Nellie recognised that she had no earthly chance in a race with these, and acted accordingly. When we were on the fields she was invariably loose when the other dogs were held back. She was our finder. When a hare bolted Nellie followed it, but if she saw a pair of thoroughbreds shoot by her she at once took things easy. She knew that a stout old hare would take all the fire out of young dogs before it had been turned very often, and so she reserved herself until they began to get exhausted. Then at the right moment she joined the chase, with a vigour and fury of onset which must have been astonishing to the unfortunate hare, and generally secured the prize which others had done so much to earn. This trick was often repeated, and never failed to draw laughter and admiring cheers from our gang. Does not this show reasoning power? At home she was constantly giving proofs that she understood what was said by the members of the family. If this book could claim to be a contribution to physiology, I would give many further facts in proof that at least one animal can reason.

Nellie was bred in a curious way. Her mother was what the "fancy" would term *an accident*, and was a cross between a prize bull-bitch and a well-bred Gordon setter. Her father was a greyhound. It is not generally known that the pure-bred bulldog possesses the sense of smell in almost if not quite as high a degree as the bloodhound. Nellie's nose power was as amazing as it was sometimes amusing, and would have been altogether incredible to me had I not witnessed it. She could run on my scent quite readily, even in the suburbs of London, and when I rode in a trap.

One Sunday when I went for a drive in a pony-trap. Nellie was left at home, much to her disgust, for she always exhibited more resentment at being left behind on a Sunday than on a week-day. Our trips to the country always took place on Saturday night or Sunday morning. On the occasion in question I drove twelve miles without stopping, and then pulled up for refreshment. In about ten minutes' time I was astonished to see Nellie approaching me, making curious grimaces, as if attempting to excuse herself. At first I thought that she had managed to get out immediately after I started, and had kept me in sight all along, but when I reached home I learned that she had been detained quite twenty minutes after my departure, and escaped when the door was opened to a visitor.

Another time Cardiff and I were crossing, in the daytime, a preserve which was so strictly watched that it was quite impossible to get a run there without being seen, and as all the keepers knew us, and had had us fined more than once, we put all the dogs on the lead, including Nellie. We were walking along a footpath where there was a right of way, when suddenly Nellie became extremely restless, and it was evident that she scented a hare, as she tried to get off in a particular direction. The field was perfectly level, and had been browsed quite bare by sheep. We stood and looked well and long, but could see no hare. We knew that Nellie never made a mistake, and that the hare must be somewhere near us. They sometimes lie so close, and take such advantage of the slightest inequality of the ground, that it is very difficult to see them. And so we continued to stand and look. Cardiff was highly amused, and said, "Where on earth can she be?" He then suggested that he should hold all the other dogs, and that I should allow Nellie to lead me to the hare. I agreed, and Nellie led me forward in a perfectly straight line. The field was large, and she led me so far that I began to think that she must be at fault. I noticed, however, that the farther we travelled the more eager she became and the more stealthy her movements. At length the hare bolted. I measured, by stepping it, the distance from where she lay back to the path, and found it to be two hundred and thirty-two yards.

When Nellie was about six weeks old she fell into the hands of a poacher named Smith. He began to take her out when she was nine months old, and very soon she became known as the best lurcher in Kent. At night she caught hares and rabbits, and in the daytime pheasants and even partridges among the bushes and the bracken. Of course she retrieved everything she caught, and any one, except her master, who attempted to take her game away fared badly. Many times have we known her when carrying back a hare, and finding herself confronted by a keeper and one or two dogs, put down the hare, fight and rout the enemy, and then pick up her prize and calmly trot back to me as if nothing remarkable had happened. The only thing in the world that can frighten her is a gun. When she sees one in the hands of a stranger she cannot be induced to go near him. It is my belief that she must at some time of her life have seen a dog shot.

She came into my possession in a curious way. Her first master, Smith, had her at work one night when she was nearly two years old, driving rabbits to nets. A keeper watched him for a considerable time, and at a favourable moment began to lift the nets. Soon the two men were face to face, the keeper with a bundle of nets across his arm. Finding himself outwitted, the poacher said, "Let me have my nets and I'll go away." The keeper answered, "You may go, but you'll go without the nets." Thereupon the two men began fighting. The keeper was accompanied by a large black retriever, and the two dogs began fighting also. The terrible fangs and agility of the hound and the reckless courage of the bulldog soon placed victory on Nellie's side. The retriever was killed. Then she turned her attention to her master's opponent, and attacked him so furiously that in a very short time he howled for mercy, yielded up the nets, and Nellie and her master walked off. Several months later the poacher was sitting in his garden one Sunday morning reading a newspaper. The keeper, who happened to be passing, recognised him. No words were exchanged, but a few days later a summons came. At the hearing the keeper swore that Smith set the dog on to him, and the sentence was one of four months' imprisonment. Whilst Smith was in jail some nephews of his who lived three or four miles away began to take Nellie out at night, but their mother took alarm lest they should share the fate of their uncle, and gave out privately that she was for sale. I heard of this, and on going to purchase her was surprised to have her offered me as a gift on condition that I would never allow her to come into that district again. It appears that the poacher's wife planned the whole affair in the hope that when he came out of prison, and found himself without a dog, he would take to ordinary work. This explanation was not given me until long afterwards.

The first time I took Nellie into the country I was met at a certain railway station by Hyde, to whom I had written the day before. He took a long look at the latest addition to the pack, and then looking me full in the face, said, "Do you know what you have got there?" I said I did not know exactly, and asked him what he thought of her. He replied, "She is the best lurcher in England, and you'll find her catch more hares than all the other dogs together." Within ten minutes she had caught a hare, in fact she caught one on the very first field we came to. On that day we had a long walk, in the course of which we bagged eight hares and three rabbits, all of them found, and most caught, by Nellie. Over and over again did Hyde stand and express, in the most forcible terms, his admiration of the way in which she worked the fields. Before night he exacted from me a solemn promise that if she ever had puppies he should have one. In short, we had at last got just the dog we wanted. She worked the fields exactly as her grandfather, the setter, might have done, and combined with all the stamina and tenacity of the bulldog a good deal of the speed of the greyhound. When she came off a field one might wager a kingdom to an orange that there was not even a rat alive on it. If she had a fault, it was that her nose was too good. She not only scented her prey at almost incredible distances, but located it so exactly that she was constantly catching hares and rabbits before they bolted. We often had to console ourselves for the absence of sport by reflecting on the fullness of our bag.

When I had acquired this treasure I was acquainted with a young man whose father farmed about six hundred acres of land in Surrey. About half-a-dozen times every season small coursing parties met there. I had an invitation to attend one, and my friend suggested that in addition to a couple of greyhounds I should take Nellie, as only a few dogs would be present, and we were sure to get running enough for all. By one of those unaccountable strokes of ill-fortune with which all coursers are familiar, two whole hours were spent in ranging the fields without a single hare being put up. The company were growing tired and impatient, and several expressed doubts as to there being any hares there at all. At length my friend suggested that Nellie should be turned loose, and that the slipper should follow her up as closely as possible. He urged that if there was anything on the ground she would find it, and that a course or two subject to her interference would be better than none. The party agreed, and Nellie was loosed. In about two minutes she had found a hare, but, sad to say, she had also caught it without a run. She dashed at it as it lay in some rushes, and although it attempted to bolt, she gripped it before it got under way. She amused some members of the party, and made others exchange knowing looks, by retrieving the hare and placing it at my feet. Starting off again, she quickly found another hare, which she pulled out of a bush. Within ten minutes of being turned loose she had caught four. By this time the sportsmen of the party had begun to object and I then put her on the lead. She had, at any rate, demonstrated that the place was not without hares, and we had a very fair day's sport afterwards.

Although the hunting instinct is stronger in her than in any animal I have ever known, she can repress it at times, as the following incident will prove. A friend of mine had induced me to lend him Nellie for a day with the rabbits. He took her thirty-four miles into the country by train to a place she had never seen before. When he loosed her on the fields, instead of searching for rabbits as he urged and expected, she started for home, and knocked at our door (she always knocks like a human being) almost exactly two hours after she had been released.

Before I acquired Nellie we had to walk every field we came to in order to ascertain if it contained a hare; afterwards we never needed to do more than stand on a hillock and watch her range it. All the other dogs got accustomed to seeing everything bolt in front of her, and so they scarcely ever attempted to use their noses, but simply followed her up, trusting to her. From the day of her arrival she has been the leader of the pack.

Once in the early morning she caught two hares, and as most of the fields around were ploughed and the ground was wet, Greenman and Cardiff, who were with me, suggested that I should wait at a certain stile whilst they gave two or three runs to some young dogs. The place swarmed with hares, and so they did not need Nellie's services. The stile was at the corner of a field, and for some reason or other a number of the hares they disturbed came my way. When they returned I had beside me a heap of hares, seventeen in number, all caught by Nellie. We could only carry away nine, and so we hid the others in some bushes, and they were collected by Hyde on the following night. This was her largest haul, but on many occasions she caught as many as eight and ten. Considering how many we should have missed had we not had her, it is scarcely too much to say that three-fourths of our total spoil is due to her. I have never known her show the least sign of fatigue. Considering the pace at which she went, she must often have covered a hundred miles in a day, yet she invariably tried the last bush we passed. In fighting—men or dogs—she exhibited the same tenacity of purpose.

A greyhound bitch of mine, a companion of Nellie's, had a litter of whelps, and Nellie *ought* to have whelped about the same time. She had already had three litters, but was not allowed to have any this time. A day or two after the youngsters arrived I noticed that Nellie took an immense interest in them. I visited them three or four times a day for the purpose of feeding the mother, and each time Nellie made strenuous efforts to enter their compartment, but fearing the dam would attack her, I kept her out. On one occasion, however, she whined most piteously, and altogether conducted herself in such a manner as induced me to take a couple of the babies outside and place them on some straw beside her. I was under the impression that she wanted simply to lick them, but I found, greatly to my astonishment, that she wanted to wet-nurse them. She was full of milk, and eventually nursed nearly the whole litter. She weighed about fifty-eight pounds, and so was, of course, much bigger and stronger than the mother.

Let me here place on record a fact which, when stated, has caused me to be laughed at more than once, but to which I hold. I have noticed within myself a strange feeling in relation to Nellie. When I am accompanied by other dogs I *feel* that they are but dogs; with Nellie I feel that I am in presence of a reasoning being. The consideration which mind must ever extort from mind I cannot withhold from her.

I am sure the reader will be glad to learn that my Nellie—my glorious Nellie—is still alive, and that although age has diminished her speed and somewhat dimmed her vision, she is still able to spoil a landlord or to fight a keeper.

MY NELLIE
Come with me and with my Nellie,
Ere the lazy sun is up,
Over hill and over hollow,
See her move and never stop;
See her plough the tangled bracken,
Search the bushes and the wood,
When the cunning hare has bolted,
Watch her light foot touch the sod.

All the week in smoke and bother,
Do we smother, she and I;
Sunday morning brings us leisure,
Purer air and clearer sky.
Oh, how joyous is the journey
To the flower and the tree;
In the wild wood we are happy,
On the hillside we are free.

XXVIII

BLUCHER

IS MOTHER was a German boar-hound, and, he was born on the sixty-fifth anniversary of the battle of Quatre Bras, and so we called him Blucher. At once he justified his title. Almost as soon as his eyes opened he began to bully his brothers and sisters, and in a few months' time he mastered the pack. His father was a mongrel—three-quarters greyhound and one-quarter bulldog. If anybody wants a dog for all-round poaching purposes, I should advise him to breed it in a similar way. With such an animal the poacher is safe, for it will fight an army of keepers, and by reason of its wonderful quickness and terrible jaws, do more damage than six bulldogs.

Blucher was not vicious in the ordinary sense of the term. He would allow children to pull his legs from under him, and fall atop of him in the street, and he was always most playful. He never bit a human being except at the right time, if I may use the phrase. He did not always wait to be set on, but he was always so nearly in the right that it was difficult, if not impossible, to condemn him. By way of illustrating this I may give an incident which occurred when he was quite young, and presumably not so sensible as he afterwards became.

A family consisting of three persons, father, mother, and daughter, living next door to me, were very fond of Blucher. They fed him from the first day he was able to lap milk, and, in fact, he spent nearly as much time on their premises as on mine. When the puppy was a few months old the daughter was married, and instead of leaving the house of her parents, took her husband to live there. In due course a baby arrived, and from the first Blucher took an immense interest in it. He was never so happy as when allowed to lick its face, and he would sit for hours watching it as it lay in the cradle. A nursemaid was engaged, and when she took it out for an airing Blucher invariably accompanied them. It happened that the flagged footway in front of our houses was very wide, and sloped somewhat towards the street, along which a tramway ran. One day the nurse placed the baby in a perambulator, which she wheeled out on the flagstones, and having somewhat incautiously left it standing crosswise, with its front wheel facing the street, returned indoors for shopping orders. In all probability Blucher touched the machine, for it moved forward towards the road, and having its pace accelerated by the descent at the kerbstone, never stopped until it stood right across the tramway. Immediately afterwards a tramcar came along, and of course the driver was obliged to pull up. The conductor dismounted and attempted to remove the obstruction, but the moment he placed his hand on it he received a bite from Blucher which caused him to withdraw rather hastily. Then the driver dismounted and tried coaxing, but with no effect. Losing his temper, he lashed the dog savagely with his whip, and was so well bitten in return that during the remainder of the interview he stood on the farther end of the car. By this time a small crowd had collected, and many tried their powers of persuasion, but the only result was that Blucher became more enraged, waltzed round the perambulator, and kept the people at a distance. Then a policeman appeared. He pushed his way through the crowd, but before he could reach the baby he in his turn was bitten. Furious at finding the representative of the law set at defiance, he kicked out energetically in the direction of the dog, but hit nothing. For each fruitless kick he dealt Blucher managed to place two or three highly effective bites. The situation was becoming extremely interesting when the return of the nurse spoiled all the fun. She seized the perambulator and wheeled it away, accompanied by Blucher, who wagged his tail and seemed highly pleased. There was much talk of summonses after this mishap, but none took effect. The policeman called at my house and threatened dreadful things, but he afterwards allowed himself to be persuaded by the neighbours to let the matter drop. Everybody knew that the dog was not vicious, and his conduct on this occasion won him many fresh friends. Indeed, for a good many months little boys and girls kept calling with packages of broken meat and other dainties, which were usually left with the explanation, "Please ma'am, mother says this is for the dog that guarded the baby."

We began to take him out when he was nine months old, and he soon mastered his work. I had taught him to retrieve long before that by means of a ball of worsted. When he fetched it back I petted and stroked him, and made him feel extremely pleased with himself. After a time he would allow none of the other dogs to bring back anything, but constituted himself sole retriever of the pack, and insisted on doing this part of the work, even if he had to fight for it. An amusing illustration of his mastery in this respect was afforded when one Sunday evening three of us were out in Kent together—Greenman, Cardiff, and I. We were walking along a road which was new to us, and came to a lane which branched off sharply to the left. About three hundred yards down this lane, and on the right, there lay a wood. A field intervened between the wood and our road. The time was near to nightfall, and we could see that a great many rabbits had already emerged from the wood. We reasoned that if we returned to the lane after dark, and released the dogs at the corner of the wood, they would rush along the field and intercept the rabbits, many of which would by that time be some distance away from home. We acted as we had planned, returned back to the lane, went down it in the dark, and loosed the dogs, which shot through the hedge and along the edge of the wood. In less than a minute Blucher brought back a rabbit. He placed it at my feet, and I stroked him, and, waving my hand towards the field, said, "Go on, Blucher." He went off again, and in a very short time returned with another. After a word or two of encouragement he again darted forward and fetched a third. This performance was repeated until we had seven rabbits lying on the road. It happened that at this time Cardiff had a young greyhound in the pack which he had taken great pains to teach retrieving. When he saw the little heap of rabbits on the road, all of which had been fetched by Blucher, he began to feel suspicious, and remarking, "I can't understand how it is that my dogs don't catch anything," scrambled over the fence. Before he had gone very far he met his own educated dog carrying a rabbit towards us, but at that moment Blucher approached, seized the prize, and triumphantly bore it away. I shall not soon forget the mixture of amusement and indignation with which Cardiff announced to us that Blucher was a —— thief, and that he believed that his dogs had caught all the rabbits.

About this time we were in the habit of hiring a small two-horse brake and driving into the country on Sundays. The party generally numbered from eight to a dozen, with about as many dogs. On one occasion as we drove along I saw a hare on a field, and asked the driver to pull up, so that I might dismount and chase it. I took two dogs with me, one of which was Blucher. The hare made for a wood at the opposite side of the field, but was caught just before it reached it. Almost immediately a keeper dashed out, and seizing the hare, attempted to pull it away from Blucher. The dog, however, held on tight to his prize. The keeper raised a stick which he was carrying and dealt the dog a heavy blow along the ribs, which made him yell. Blucher released the hare, but immediately flew at the keeper, and bit him so severely about the arms and neck that he soon threw the hare on the ground and ran. After a parting bite or two Blucher picked the hare up and galloped with it over to me. The brake was hidden from the keeper's view by an intervening hill, but after I reached it we drove along the road until we reached a point at which we could see and be seen. Then we observed the keeper stripped of his clothes, including his shirt, and evidently examining his wounds. We gave him a rousing cheer as a parting salute and drove away.

One of our most amusing experiences was the following. It occurred when Blucher was very young, but not before he was full grown, a very big dog, weighing ninety-six pounds. About six of us were down in Surrey one Saturday night, and walking along a road with which we were but slightly acquainted. Three of the dogs, including Blucher, were loose, and were working the fields on either hand. The night was very still and warm, and we were moving slowly. Presently we heard a most fearful screaming. We strained our ears, but could not recognise the voice of any particular animal. The uproar was a succession of most pitiful shrieks, mingled with angry yells of deeper tone, as if three or four animals of different sorts were all being tortured together. The noise drew nearer, but obviously the movement in our direction was extremely slow. After listening for some minutes we became impatient, and, crossing the field, met Blucher dragging along a goat. He had never seen one before, and evidently thought it legitimate game. The goat was of the male sex, and was about three-quarters grown. He had horns as sharp as needles, and in addition to protesting by word of mouth in the energetic manner I have described, he used his weapons with such effect that Blucher's skin over the ribs was a collection of punctures. Indeed, I do not believe that in all his subsequent encounters he received anything like the number of wounds inflicted by the horns of that goat. I had to rub ointment over him for two or three weeks afterwards, and we all agreed that although Billy must ultimately have succumbed, he made a most heroic if noisy defence, and that when he escaped he had earned all the honours of war.

Blucher could not endure black retrievers. In the south of England most keepers go their rounds accompanied by these dogs, which are supposed to be plucky and reliable guards. Whenever we met a keeper there was naturally an exchange of high words, if nothing worse. This excited Blucher, and if the man happened to be accompanied by a dog he invariably fought and killed it, nor did it take him, as a rule, more than a minute or two to complete the operation. At an early age his hatred of the whole retriever tribe became a positive mania. He condemned them, I suppose, because of the bad company that some of them kept, and wherever he met them he slew them. This weakness became very inconvenient to me, because not only did he attack them in the London streets, but he even followed them into their own homes and finished them there.

On several occasions I had to pay damages for these exploits. I remember one day as I walked along Queen's Road, Peckham, a black retriever came out of a gate about fifty yards ahead. Blucher dashed at it, but when he reached it, instead of catching hold, he by some mischance slipped and fell. He must have nipped it, because the animal howled, and shot across the lawn in front of its owner's villa, and indoors, closely followed by Blucher. The retriever ran upstairs and took refuge in a bedroom, but only to be attacked and killed by Blucher there. Its howls were most dreadful, and the shrieks of the mistress of the house, her grown-up daughter, and a maidservant were heart-rending. I stood on the doorstep and shouted and whistled, but all to no purpose. In the middle of the din a gardener from a neighbouring house arrived, and after arming himself with a poker slammed the hall door in my face, leaving me outside. "Now," said he, "I have him." I shouted to him to keep his hands off the dog or else he would rue it, but as I could not get in I believed that Blucher's days were numbered. My suspense was not of long duration. When Blucher had finished his business upstairs he came down, and seeing the front door closed, and a man standing there with a poker in his hand, he entered the drawing-room and jumped clean through the plate-glass window. I examined him afterwards, and did not find even a scratch. I need hardly add that I cleared out of that lawn very quickly, and did not visit the neighbourhood again for some considerable time.

On another day I was walking along some very rough streets

in the lower part of Deptford, accompanied by Blucher, who was some yards behind me. Turning a corner, I came upon a small crowd, in the centre of which were two men stripped and fighting. I felt no inclination to look on, especially as I had some business in hand, and so I pushed through the outer fringe and walked away. Before I had gone far I became aware of a tremendous commotion behind me, and looking back, saw Blucher attacking the two pugilists. He repeatedly transferred his attentions from the one to the other, and as they were nearly naked, punished them so severely about the arms that they fairly howled with pain. A dozen policemen would not have scattered the crowd so quickly. The men took refuge in the houses, and I blew my whistle and ran up the street, followed by Blucher. My explanation of his conduct is that in coming suddenly upon the crowd he concluded too hastily that the men were fighting me.

One of his feats brought me the thanks of at least a dozen people. A certain wealthy gentleman kept a bull-terrier which lay on his lawn in fine weather, and was a nuisance to all who had occasion to call there. Hidden among shrubs, when anybody came inside the gate this dog crept noiselessly out to attack them. The owner was always profuse in apologies, and ready to pay hush-money to those who were bitten, and so the brute escaped. Among the sufferers was a postman, who was bitten twice. He was compensated handsomely on both occasions, but he became so nervous that whenever his duty compelled him to call at that house he felt quite ill. He implored me to allow Blucher to interview the offender, and I consented. We visited the place one evening at dusk, and nobody has ever been bitten there since. The blood of that bull-terrier besprinkled his master's doorstep.

Blucher always did his retrieving in the most tender manner, but occasionally, when he had been out many hours, and felt extremely hungry, he devoured a rabbit, crunching its bones with the greatest ease. I have even known him to consume nearly the whole of a hare. Of course this occurred very seldom, and only when circumstances justified such conduct. Once he was out with me in the London streets during the whole of a long day. I offered him food before starting, but he ate very little. In the evening I mounted an omnibus with the intention of going home, and before we had gone very far had my attention drawn by my fellow passengers to the fact that my dog was carrying a shoulder of mutton. It was partially covered with mud, and as nobody knew where it came from, there was no reason why we should deprive him of it. His plan was to place it on the ground and eat away until the bus was a considerable distance ahead, when he would pick up his prize and gallop in front of the bus for another feed. Long before we reached home he had picked every morsel of meat off the bone, greatly to the astonishment and amusement of my fellow-passengers.

It goes without saying that Blucher was not equal in speed to a thoroughbred greyhound, but there were very few hares indeed that could outrun him, and he was wonderfully clever at catching. In nine courses out of ten a greyhound ran with him, and when the thoroughbred reached the hare first, and caused it to swing round, Blucher seldom failed to grip it. On his merits as an all-round poacher's friend and companion he was much admired by the fraternity. At last he grew old, and I was induced to part with him to a near neighbour of mine who prized him much and pro-vided him with a comfortable home. Even then he distinguished himself. His owner, an elderly man, when out a little way in the country one evening, was attacked by two sturdy tramps, who attempted to rob him; but Blucher nearly killed them both. The police traced their blood for a long distance next morning, but after all Blucher's master refused to prosecute, on the ground that they had been sufficiently punished already. He remained with this man until he died of old age. Peace be to his ashes!

XXIX

TAFF

THOUGH POACHING DOGS are not, as a rule, thoroughbred greyhounds, one of the breed is always a useful member of a pack because of his superior speed, and occasionally he may be found to be the most valuable of all. Everything
depends on individual characteristics and early training.

To win stakes on a coursing field a dog must display little or
no intelligence. He must pursue the hare as a matter of pure
instinct, and even such a small offence as "cutting off corners" is
a disqualification.

There is a story told of a cockney angler who, on being discovered doing something illegal, explained that "when he went
fishing he wanted to catch fish". There are greyhounds built in a
similar way—when they go hunting they want to catch hares, and
they do not always proceed according to the strict rules of coursing. Some dogs are cunning almost from birth, and some are
made so by early mismanagement. Almost any dog may be made
useless for legitimate coursing by being allowed to chase rabbits
(which run in an entirely different manner from hares) or even
hares if he be allowed to pursue them before he is full grown. It
was in this way that "Taff" was spoilt.

Taff, as we called him, or Steam Jacket as he was registered in
the "Greyhound Stud Book", was a grandson of the famous
Misterton, who won in stakes and earned in stud fees over £16,000

for his master. Taff was bred by a member of the National Coursing Club, who is now dead, and need not be named. It is sufficient to say that in the year of Taff's birth his owner raised a very large number of whelps. Having more than he could accommodate on his own premises, he "planted out" a considerable number with friends and acquaintances. When this is done it is always clearly understood that the young dogs are not to be allowed to see a hare or a rabbit until their owner decides on having them "tried".

Taff, and the litter to which he belonged, were placed with a small farmer near Seven-oaks in Kent, who had two sons aged respectively fifteen and seventeen years. The father had a contract from the local authority for repairing all the roads in his district, and was necessarily absent from the farm during a considerable part of his time.

The neighbourhood swarmed with game, and, as might be expected, the youths yielded to the temptation to indulge in some sport. When the young greyhounds were of the right age their owner decided on viewing them. With that object he one day took train to the station nearest their domicile, which lay about half a mile off the main road. Proceeding up the lane in the direction of the little farm-house he encountered one of the youths already alluded to. After the usual salutation, Mr. Blank inquired—

"How are the puppies?" To which the engaging rustic responded frankly—

"Oh, first rate, sir. They *can* catch hares, and no mistake."

"Indeed!" said Mr. Blank, a little surprised. "May I ask how many they have caught?"

The youth replied, "Oh, the number is past counting, sir. Why, the red dog alone has caught dozens. He is by far the best of the lot."

The red dog was Taff. When, a little later, the saplings were tried it was found that they all "ran cunning", to use a phrase known to the fraternity. Taff was found to be extremely fast.

Indeed, competent judges are of opinion today that he was the fastest dog of the Misterton strain, and it is quite an open question whether any greyhound ever exceeded him in speed. Yet he never won a shilling in stakes. When slipped at a hare he invariably led his opponent by from ten to twenty lengths in a long run up, but when he neared his game, instead of dashing at it in the orthodox manner, he slowed down so as to be able to turn quickly when the hare turned, instead of being thrown out many yards, as all dogs are when they fail to catch.

It was not uncommon to see a dog which had been beaten ridiculously in the race from the slips pass by Taff and score the turn when the hare was approached. There was only one way of getting an honest run out of Taff. This was managed by keeping him on the lead, and allowing him to look on whilst five or six hares were being caught by other dogs. By that time he had generally become so eager that he forgot his cunning, and ran true, at least until three or four turns had been taken. We practised this trick when anybody had a young dog that he considered very speedy, and it was admitted that if any youngster could come near holding his own with "Old Potboiler" in the matter of speed he was fit to travel all over the world. But Taff never met his equal. I have a vivid remembrance of the last day on which we took him to that well-known coursing ground, the Cliffe marshes.

It was what is called a trial day. Somebody had a young dog which had simply run away from everything with which he had been previously slipped. We took the usual method of making Taff eager, and then slipped the pair at a very strong hare. Taff ran his best, and when he took the first turn was about ten lengths ahead of his opponent. Before he could swing round the latter had got in, but Taff soon caught him up and shot by him. The hare made for a gate and passed underneath it.

The weather had been wet for a week or two, and, as everybody acquainted with marsh land will understand, the ground on either side of the gate, for a distance of six or eight yards, was very sloppy. Taff rose to the jump at the beginning of the sloppy ground, and, flying over the gate, landed seven or eight yards beyond it, right on the back of the hare.

A loud laugh broke from the onlookers, and one of them called out, "—— it, he nearly jumped the field!" The owner of the rival dog was recommended to "take him home and oil his joints" and informed that he "could not run his grandfather".

There is every reason to think that had Taff not been spoilt in the manner described, he would have been worth thousands of pounds. As it was, his breeder gave him away, and after he had changed hands once or twice Cardiff purchased him for the small sum of two shillings and sixpence. It need hardly be added that henceforth his life was a busy one. Cardiff never spared himself, and his dog was likely to eat idle bread.

The splendid speed of Taff put many hares into our wallets which we should otherwise have lost. As a rule regular coursing is done on large fields, and in most cases the hare has to run a long distance before reaching cover of any sort. But large fields do not suit the poacher. He can be seen from a much greater distance when hedges are scarce. We did most of our work in small fields, and as most hares make for the nearest hedge, it will be seen that the presence of a very fast dog which could catch them up before reaching cover was a great advantage.

Taff caught most of his hares without allowing them to turn even once. He had, indeed, absolutely mastered the art of catching. He frequently bagged six and eight of a night, and came home apparently as fresh as when he started.

On one occasion a party of us was out in Kent on a Sunday. Coming to a roadside beerhouse we ordered drinks, and got into conversation with certain other people who were there. Among them was a farmer. This man informed us that there was a hare on his land which no dog could catch, and the others supported his statement. They told us that crack greyhounds had been brought long distances to course this hare, but that they had all failed to catch it. Of course we were aware that there are some hares that it is almost impossible to catch by means of dogs; but, nevertheless, someone expressed the opinion that we had a dog with us which could accomplish the feat.

The farmer thereupon offered to take us to where the hare lay, and to pay us £1 for the hare when caught, and £10 for the dog that caught it. It always lay in nearly the same place, and the farmer could distinguish it from any number of others. We allowed him to lead Taff up to it by means of a handkerchief, and when it had bolted he gave it about fifty yards' start and then released the dog. Taff turned it at once, and then caught it. The farmer stood to his offer, and still wanted to buy the dog. Cardiff, of course, refused to sell, and informed the man that the animal was to him like the Arab steed to the Dervish—unpurchasable.

Taff lived to be over ten years old, but at last, in jumping a wide stream, landed awkwardly, and hurt his back. He lingered for two or three months, but pined away, and at last died, deeply regretted by all of us.

XXX

LURCHER BREEDING

THE TERM LURCHER bears no very definite meaning, but is applied to all dogs which have in them any greyhound blood. At one time the lurcher was recognised as a distinct breed, for excellence in which prizes were offered in dog shows. But the promoters of such exhibitions soon found that it was undesirable to encourage the production of lurchers, and prizes were no longer offered. Speaking from my own experience, and without any book knowledge on the subject, I should say unhesitatingly that a cross between the greyhound and any other dog is infinitely more intelligent than either of the animals from which it is produced. There may be individual exceptions, but I am confident that this is the rule. Not only in intelligence, but in courage, a great advantage is gained by crossing.

Many people are not aware of the fact that the greyhound has qualities which are not possessed by any other dog; qualities so marked that some old authorities were of opinion that, whilst all other dogs had a common progenitor, the greyhound sprang from an original source. This is not now generally accepted, but it is undeniable that the instinct which prompts the greyhound to pursue is marvellously strong, and imparts a degree of dash, unapproached elsewhere, to any animal with a trace of it. I have never known anybody who possessed a lurcher for any considerable time who afterwards cared much for any other dog. The lurcher is good for any work which any other dog can do, and is besides capable of doing much that others cannot attempt.

In old days the lurcher was a cross between the greyhound and the collie, and there are those who still believe this cross to be the best. It is undeniably intelligent and speedy, especially if the collie be of the smooth-coated variety, which possesses more speed and much more endurance than the long-haired. But many poachers prefer a cross with the retriever. It is hardly as speedy, but its scenting power is keener, and it will almost invariably retrieve its game, which the collie cross often refuses to do. For my part, if I were using a greyhound in addition to the lurcher, I should prefer the retriever cross, but if I were working the lurcher alone, I should prefer the collie cross. There is, however, a better dog than either to be obtained by breeding in another way. Both the collie lurcher and the retriever lurcher will sometimes give tongue, and this may mean ruin to the poacher, but a dog bred as my Nellie was will never give tongue, and possesses in addition a very much better nose.

The breeder of lurchers should first of all consider what it is that he wants. The first requisites are speed, scent, and courage. Speed must be sought after in the greyhound. It exists in no other dog whatever in the necessary degree. Scent and courage are found combined in the greatest perfection in the bulldog. There is an impression abroad that the scent of the bloodhound is greater than that of any dog, but this I do not believe. I cannot imagine any scent keener than I have witnessed in the bull and modifications of the bull, a dog endowed with courage in a superlative degree, though frankness compels me to add that I have known a few thoroughbred greyhounds which were as plucky as any bulldog. The bull, too, contrary to the generally received opinion, is very intelligent and teachable. In these respects he is quite equal to the collie, retriever, or to any pure-bred dog. The conclusion to be drawn from these premises is that the ideal lurcher is a combination of bulldog and greyhound.

A first cross, however, between these two breeds will never be speedy enough to suit the poacher's purposes. In the combination the greyhound must largely predominate, as the bulldog is so slow. In developing what is required, a knowledge of the laws of breeding will greatly help and hasten the end. It may be said that, roughly, dogs follow the mother in the matter of size and the father in shape and mental characteristics. There are exceptions to this rule, as to all others, and of course the mother will always modify the shape to some extent. I would begin by taking a pure-bred greyhound bitch and putting her to a bulldog whose courage and tenacity had been proved beyond all dispute. It must be borne in mind that all bulldogs are not equally courageous or tenacious. A few are only poor fighters, and to begin with one of these would cause waste of time and failure. To use the language of the fraternity, a champion "business dog" must be procured. The puppies of this first cross will be little, if at all, faster than retrievers, but at least some of them will be as plucky as their father. Occasionally one will be found to be an arrant coward. Their mettle should be tested, and the best dog puppy selected to breed from next time. The rejected ones will make most excellent house-dogs.

The second move is to find another greyhound bitch, and put her to the dog we have selected as the best of our first cross. The puppies of this second cross will be much more speedy, but still hardly speedy enough. One of them will be found an invaluable assistant to a greyhound, but not fast enough to catch many hares by himself. He will do all the finding, and can readily work twelve hours at a stretch without feeling fatigued. To get the requisite speed it is necessary to select again the best of the litter, and have a third cross, with a pure greyhound bitch. The produce then will be practically fast enough for any purpose, and the poacher will then have just what he wants. It will be noted that the blood of the bulldog must descend in the male line, otherwise its mental qualities may be lost. I know a dog bred in this way which, although four removes from the pure-bred progenitor, yet has the head of a pure bulldog on the body of a greyhound. A good deal depends on selecting the greyhound bitches from strong and plucky strains. There are what we may call short-distance as well as long-distance greyhounds. The latter are very much to be preferred for our purpose. The bull is a very silent dog. A lurcher bred in this way will never give tongue, and because of its tenacity will in all probability retrieve without any teaching.

There is one further point to consider. If a dog is required to retrieve game over long distances he had better be as large as possible. If a hare has to be carried half a mile, the weight is too great for a dog of the size we have been considering. Some try to procure increased size by crossing with the deer-hound, but the increase in this case is very slight. Some cross with the mastiff, and get a great accession of size, but lose very much speed. The best cross for the purpose is with the German boar-hound. This will give all the size required without materially diminishing speed, and without diminishing courage in the least. The dog so obtained will readily fight a man, and that is sometimes a great consideration.

I have dealt with the matter at some length in order to make clear how the ideal lurcher may be obtained, but it must be clearly understood that a serviceable dog may generally be obtained in a less elaborate way. Some thoroughbred greyhounds are most excellent fighters. If one of these be selected, a young one by preference, and put to a German boar-hound bitch very fair lurchers of large size may be secured.

As for some purposes a large dog is needful, so for others is a small one indispensable. The professional poacher cannot afford to disdain rabbits, and these lie so close that considerable difficulty is experienced in making them bolt. If a rabbit sits in a clump of bushes or a thick brake, and sees himself surrounded by five or six greyhounds, he will think many times before coming out. As greyhounds and lurchers are too big and long-legged to penetrate bushes, the smallest dog obtainable is then of use, provided he be suitable in other respects. Most small dogs are noisy; but there is one exception, the Irish terrier, which hunts silently, and his rough coat enables him to penetrate briars, and thorn bushes where a fox terrier would probably be baffled. Here, again, a cross with the bulldog is useful, by imparting courage and endurance. I once had a little animal of sixteen pounds weight, which was three-quarters Irish terrier and one-quarter bulldog. He was very short-legged, and could penetrate brakes that other dogs could only look at. The consequence was that we obtained rabbits by the dozen where previously we had supposed they were very scarce. Tim, for such was his name, never emitted a sound, but his route would have been apparent to a blind man by the screams of the unfortunate rabbits on which he inflicted capital punishment. He was poisoned at last. In the case of these small dogs speed must be left out of account altogether. It cannot be obtained apart from long legs, and long legs are just what we must avoid.

XXXI

A POACHING PUSS

THERE IS NO REASON why one of the boldest and most successful poachers ever encountered by the writer should be refused notice for the sole reason that he was a cat. The litter of kittens to which he belonged first saw the light at a small farm-house where the kitchen-garden was surrounded by a ditch and an embankment honeycombed with rabbit-holes. The kittens were born in summer, and when weaned were all given away to people at a distance, except one, a tom. At first milk was plentiful, and Thomas fared sumptuously many times every day; but all acquainted with life in outlying farm-houses, where milk is not produced for sale, will know that during the winter months it is often scarce, and sometimes unprocurable. This was the case in the farm-house in question during Tom's first winter, while fresh meat, except in the form of fowl, was seldom seen. And so it came to pass that at the age of five months or thereabouts Tom found himself reduced to vegetarian diet. This was not at all to his taste, as the grimaces with which he munched cabbage and porridge plainly showed. He was still small enough to penetrate rabbit-holes with ease, and he soon began to prey on the baby bunnies.

When he seized one he generally brought it indoors and feast-ed on it leisurely. Sometimes he was not able to eat the whole of it, but whatever remained was soon disposed of by his mother. The first result of this luxurious living was an extraordinary increase in Tom's size. This was so considerable that in a very short time he was quite unable to enter the rabbit-holes. He then altered his tactics, and crouched just above the mouths of the holes, and pounced on the rabbits as they came out. After a time the rabbits almost deserted the embankment around the garden, and Tom was obliged to hunt farther afield, and he often roamed a mile or more from home. About this time the rabbit diet seemed to become precarious. At any rate, whether from choice or necessity, Tom took to catching birds. Not only did such small game as sparrows and finches attract his attention, but blackbirds and even wood-pigeons occasionally provided him with a relish. Of course rabbits still formed his most frequent dish, and by this time he was able to catch them by springing on them in the long grass. Another and more ingenious artifice of his was sitting on the branches of trees under which rabbits were playing. When one sat right under him, or nearly so, he dropped on it like a stone, often from a height of thirty feet. Of course he was not able to eat a full-grown rabbit at one meal, and soon he formed the habit of hiding the part which remained. Sometimes he buried this in the loose mould of the garden, but more frequently he simply scratched a place for it in the nearest heap of straw. Now and again an intolerable stench was noticed in barn, or stable, or hay-loft, and when search was made part of a rabbit was found in an advanced stage of decomposition. Tom always did his hunting through the night, and slept during the daytime. In cold weather he lay as near the fire as possible, and often through utter weariness and repletion he submitted to being trodden on without moving.

By the time Tom was eighteen months old he was bigger than two ordinary cats, and his coat was beautifully silky and clean. Experience has since taught me that all cats which are compelled to get their own living at an early age grow to a surprising size. Of course this does not happen in towns, but it is my firm opinion that to feed cats at all freely in the country after they have reached the age of six months is mistaken kindness near akin to cruelty.

When Tom was two and a half years old the family removed to a fresh neighbourhood, fifteen miles away, and with the household goods and chattels Tom was carted to the new abode enclosed in a hamper wrapped in paper, so that he might not see the route. Contrary to expectation, he made no attempt to return to his old home, as many less travelled pussies succeed in doing. In a day or two he was quite reconciled to his new surroundings, and no check was placed on his movements. It so happened that there was a wood of nearly four hundred acres in extent, with very thick undergrowth, within five hundred yards of the new home, which formed part of a game preserve of some four thousand acres. On the third night after Tom's arrival he brought home a pheasant before 10 P.M., showing that he must have visited the wood. Almost every night after that he brought home something. Partridges were frequent prizes, but much smaller birds, such as thrushes and blackbirds, appeared to satisfy him just as well. He never left home until nightfall, and when he caught anything, however small, he returned for the night. Most cats which take to poaching become more or less wild, but Tom remained as sociable, gentle, and harmless as before. During the four and a half years which his life in the new quarters covered, he must have killed many hundred pheasants and partridges. Had he gone wild he would have lived in the wood in the daytime, and would probably have been shot at an early stage of his career, but through coming home when his work was finished he escaped.

However, the luckiest life must end sometime, and at last Tom was missed. He was called and inquired after for several days, all to no purpose; and his absence gave great concern to the lady members of the family. More than a month passed before any tidings were heard of him, and then the sad news of his fate reached the ears of his friends. It so happened that the head-gamekeeper over the preserve in which Tom operated lived some three miles away in what had once been a farm-house. Near it were some ruined stables and cowsheds. A gable faced the public road, and on this the keeper was in the habit of nailing the birds and beasts of prey which he destroyed. On the strength of information received, the lady members of the family paid this wall a visit one fine morning, and were thrown into paroxysms of inconsolable grief on discovering there, nailed up among the carcasses of carrion-crows, hawks, weasels, and stoats, the form of their beloved Tom. That keeper was compelled to endure a trying half-hour, in which he was made to feel thoroughly ashamed of having ever been born. But strong language could not bring poor Tom back to life.

XXXII

THE POACHERS'
PROTECTION FUND

APPLICATIONS FOR admission into our gang were frequently made by people who had heard of our adventures, but we soon learned that it was necessary to refuse the great majority of these. Sometimes a pathetic appeal would be made by an enthusiast to be allowed to come out even once, and occasionally we agreed to give an applicant a trial, but one of these would-be recruits nearly got several of us into serious trouble. He was a boxer in his way, and being very ambitious of shining in the fistic art, had taken lessons at the academy of the well-known Jack Wannop. During the ramble in which he accompanied us we met a keeper who seemed inclined to be quarrelsome. In accordance with our general practice we tried to avoid a fight, and all except the new recruit walked quietly away. He remained behind, bandying words with the keeper, notwithstanding our repeated appeals to him to come on. When we were about two hundred yards away we noticed that the men were fighting. Feeling sure that the keeper would soon find himself outclassed, and give in, we still moved slowly away. It was obvious at an early stage that the keeper was getting the worst of the encounter, but he stood up pluckily to his work. Presently he received a knock-down blow, and soon after another of the same sort. After that the fight was a very one-sided affair. The keeper kept retreating, and was followed up by the other, who knocked him down again and again. Presently the stage was reached at which the keeper did not desire to continue the fight, but his opponent refused to stop. Over and over again he pulled the man up on his feet only to knock him down the next moment. At last two of us went back and stopped what had now become a disgraceful exhibition. Finding the keeper with his eyes bunged up, and beaten black and blue, we pulled the boxer away, and walked quickly off for a mile or more. Then we started two or three hares, which absorbed our attention, and we failed to notice that we were being followed. When, an hour or two later, we reached a railway station, and took train for London, the person or persons who had kept us in sight ascertained the station to which we had booked and telegraphed to the police, who met us as we alighted, and demanded our names and addresses. The upshot was that the keeper swore before the magistrates that we had all three assaulted him, feeling perhaps ashamed to admit that one man had thrashed him so severely. It was almost a case for imprisonment, but eventually we got off with fines and costs, which amounted to over £5 each. This showed us the necessity for establishing a fund on which we could draw in such cases of emergency, and led to the formation of "The Poachers' Protection Fund"; at first we agreed to subscribe a shilling a week, but we soon found that sixpence a week was more than sufficient. A considerable number of people paid into the fund who very seldom accompanied us in our journeys to the country, and in all we had nearly twenty members, so that in a few months we had a considerable sum in hand.

We made Hyde a free member. This was the least we could do, as we were in the habit of calling at his house at all hours of the day and night. He was fined pretty frequently before there was any fund to fall back on, and more frequently afterwards. Leaving Hyde's fines out of account, two pence a week would have covered all our liabilities quite easily. It will thus be seen that the pecuniary risk involved in poaching is not very great. Imprisonment may be avoided almost always by the poacher drawing the line at assault. The case may stand differently in remote country districts, but in the neighbourhood of London the magistrates, who are mostly game preservers, are literally afraid to inflict the maximum penalties for offences against the Game Laws. The democratic press, by scrutinising and exposing harsh sentences on poachers, instills a wholesome terror into the minds of the privileged land monopolists. I myself have stood in a police court whilst a keeper made an application for a summons against a poacher, and heard the magistrates' clerk, who doubtless obeyed the instructions of his superiors, refuse to grant it except under a statute which made the maximum penalty for the offence a fine of £2.

As I had more time on my hands than any other member of the gang, the task of attending court to pay fines generally fell to me. The hearing almost always came off in the police courts of Kent or Surrey, and Hyde was almost always the defendant. It was amusing to watch the air of surprise with which the court officials, as well as the county police and gamekeepers, viewed the stranger who stepped forward when sentence was pronounced and paid the money.

When I could not attend my place was always taken by another member of the gang, who was the owner of eight public houses. This man, whom we will call Mr. Blackheath, was an extensive breeder of greyhounds, and well known in the coursing world. He always declared that he would rather have one night's poaching than a whole season's legitimate coursing. He was an athlete of remarkable powers, and the long night walks which poaching furnished enabled him to work off some of his superfluous energy. When he came out with us attired in tight-fitting corduroys, reefer jacket, and peaked cap, it was difficult to believe that he was the same individual who in the daytime sported a tall hat, sealskin waistcoat, diamond-decked finger-rings, and spotless outfit. He made us laugh by relating an incident which occurred when, arrayed in all the glory of his stylish attire, he went to pay one of Hyde's fines. Stepping forward when sentence was pronounced, he drew from his pocket a sealskin purse and poured into the palm of his hand a quantity of gold. The gamekeepers looked at the police, the police looked at the magistrates, and the magistrates looked at one another. An old keeper expressed the feeling of all present by blurting out, "—— me, the poachers are getting respectable."

On another day I went down to a town in Surrey in response to a letter from Mrs. Hyde. A few minutes after I reached the police court Hyde's case was called. Two keepers swore that they saw him ferreting rabbits. When they had given their evidence the Chairman of the Bench, to whom Hyde was well known, inquired "Hyde, do you ever do any work?"

"Certainly I do," replied Hyde: "was I not at work when these two perishers interrupted me?"

"I mean," said the magistrate, "do you ever do any *honest* work?"

"No, no," said Hyde; "what you mean to ask is whether I ever work twelve or fourteen hours a day for twelve shillings a week. My answer is no, and I don't intend to do so. I can always live on three rabbits a week, and as long as my luck holds good I will get more than that."

"You are fined £1 and costs," was the answer.

The Poachers' Protection Fund was a tower of strength to our gang. By stopping short of assault we kept within the limits of illegality covered by fines, and so the poorest among us felt safe. Indeed, for years we treated many square miles of country exactly as if it belonged to us, and went over it in all directions without the slightest fear of consequences. A standing joke was to invite trustworthy friends to spend a night with us on our sporting estate, and much did they marvel at the liberties we took with comparative impunity.

XXXIII

IN PRAISE OF SPORT

DOMESTICATED ANIMALS may be regulated in their breeding, so as to be kept within any limits desired in point of number, but this can never be done with animals that are wild. The reproductive power of some animals is amazing. One pair of rabbits will produce over one hundred in a year. Indeed, a pair has been known to produce one hundred and sixty in that time. The reproductive power of hares is lower, but is still very great. It has been said, and I believe with truth, that if hares and rabbits were allowed to breed unchecked for five years, they would, by the end of that time have eaten up every blade of grass and every green thing in this country. Even the bark of trees would have disappeared. In the face of these facts the contention of those who say that we should never under any circumstances destroy life is difficult to understand. If we do not kill hares and rabbits they will kill us, by eating us out. If we are to live we must either kill them all off at once, or allow them to live and breed, and thin them down as may be necessary. Now, no one will desire to see them all killed off at once, and herein lies the justification of the sportsman. Someone must do the killing, and as animals cannot be eaten until they have first been killed, the man who denounces hunting, shooting, and fishing, and then sits down to and enjoys his dinner, is a hypocrite. The work of preparing his meal he leaves to another, and then denounces him for doing it.

Only the strict vegetarian can consistently object to taking life, and he would probably reconsider his creed if brought face to face with facts that make for starvation.

For ages our savage ancestors killed game for food, and the result is that many of us now find ourselves with an inherited hunting instinct which makes sport of this kind a very keen pleasure. A man is no more to be blamed for this feeling than is the housewife of the slum for the inherited agricultural or horticultural taste which prompts her to tend the three cracked flower-pots on her window ledge. If the hunting instinct is not allowed legitimate indulgence, it will seek gratification in more ignoble ways. No man would dream of coursing a hare or a rabbit slipped from a cage if it were open to him to find and course a free one. But the ordinary citizen seldom has a chance of coursing a wild hare unless he turns poacher. One reason for this is that so many hares are shot. It is not uncommon for a shooting-party to kill five hundred hares in a day, and this surely is not sport, and affords no test of marksmanship. Hares are generally shot in covert, where they move very slowly, and are as easy to hit as a barn-door fowl. Most shooting-parties, too, contain some novices, and a considerable proportion of the hares which are hit are not killed outright, so that anyone traversing, with terriers, ground which had been shot over the day before, may find many wounded and dying hares. A single grain of shot will generally kill a bird, or, at any rate, disable it for flying, but the hare is a strong animal, and often with a broken limb, or a fatal flesh wound, will scuttle away to die a lingering death of terror and starvation among the bushes.

The hare's defence is his speed, and to attack him in a way which does not permit of his defending himself is unsportsmanlike. Some people object to coursing on the ground that it tortures the hare with terror. Physiologists, however, inform us that great terror produces muscular paralysis, and no one has ever seen any evidence of this in the coursed hare. It is no exaggeration to say that three times out of four the hare escapes if full grown, and that he invariably hopes to escape until actually caught. When he is caught by dogs death is practically instantaneous, so that for all reasons it is much more humane to kill a hare by coursing than by shooting him.

In shooting, the best hares are as likely to get killed as the worst. In coursing the worst get caught and the best escape, and are therefore available for breeding purposes. Coursing thus operates as an artificial selection, which ensures the survival of the fittest, and the improvement of the species. If taking hares by other means than dogs were made illegal, every year would find them harder to catch, and they would soon get scattered all over the country instead of being confined to preserves as they are now.

It was stated not long ago in the House of Commons that in some parts of England a hare was as rare as an elephant. In other parts they may be counted in tens of thousands, and it is their accumulation in such enormous numbers that leads to the immense destruction of crops of which we sometimes hear. The same number of hares scattered all over the country would do no appreciable damage, and would provide an opportunity of seeing them coursed to those who are now reduced to the sickening spectacle of the worrying of caged rabbits. To catch hares by means of traps or snares is as cruel as shooting them. Netting them is a more painless process, but inspires far more terror than coursing. The conclusion to be drawn from all this is that taking hares in any other way than by means of dogs should be made illegal.

A few years ago Mr. Luttrell, M.P., introduced into the House of Commons a bill for the purpose of prohibiting the hunting, coursing, or shooting of tame or captured animals. Certain poachers talked the matter over, and whilst approving of Mr. Luttrell's object, considered that his bill did not touch the root of the evil, and therefore forwarded the following petition to another member, for presentation to the House:

THE POACHERS' PETITION

To the Right Honourable the Commons of Great Britain and Ireland

PETITION

We, the undersigned members of the Ancient Order of Poachers, respectfully address you in connection with the "Sports Bill" now before the House. Each of us can furnish you with proof of his right to speak on behalf of our Order, by referring you to records of numerous convictions for poaching and assault.

We submit—

1. That the chief difference between ourselves and orthodox sportsmen is in the clothes we wear.
2. That we take as keen an interest in the chase, and in all genuine sport, as do the Princes of the Blood, and perhaps keener.
3. That the widespread custom of organising battues for the destruction of hares is much more suggestive of the butcher than the sportsman.
4. That these vulgar orgies place the exhilarating sport of coursing beyond the reach of all except the favoured of fortune.
5. That killing hares by shooting them must always involve cruelty, in consequence of a proportion inevitably getting away wounded.
6. That taking them by means of traps or snares is cruel also.
7. That taking them by means of dogs is infinitely more humane.
8. That the latter method alone affords a test of speed and endurance in hares and dogs which entitles it to rank as sport.
9. That coursing alone ensures the survival of the fittest hares, and the consequent improvement of the breed.
10. That coursing would cause hares to disperse all over the country, so as to come within everybody's reach.
11. That such dispersal would reduce to a minimum the damage to crops of which we now frequently hear; and
12. If accompanied by the legalisation of the universal right to course, which your Honourable House can confer, would enable hard-working citizens like ourselves, who, at least, are peaceably inclined, to avoid frequent fines and imprisonment.

If your Honourable House comply with our request, your petitioners will try to relearn their prayers, in order to use them in your interest.

Then followed a number of names which need not be reproduced here.

The meaning of the word "sport" is unknown to many. A little while ago a number of motor cars were assembled at a certain place for exhibition purposes and a run into the country. Commenting on this, a leading newspaper announced next day that some gentlemen who were present "imparted a sporting character to the event by betting on the results of the run". No true sportsman could ever, by any possibility, make a bet. To strive with one's fellows in strength, speed, or endurance, is not only allowable, but ennobling. When the desire for gain creeps in, the high motive departs. No two feelings can be more utterly opposed than the manly wish to excel in honourable and friendly strife and the Shylock-like greed which wants something in return for nothing. As men grow old they cannot always remain athletes, and so are obliged to enjoy in others, or in dogs and horses, the emulation which was once their own. The most pitiable spectacle possible is that of the foolish workman, who in most cases has never visited a coursing field or a race-course, stealing into the back parlour of a public house to deposit his hard-earned money with the bookmaker. Banish, men, banish at once such meanness and folly from your minds, and with a greyhound, which you can buy for a sovereign, try an early morning on the hills. Read what was written by one of the truest sportsmen and one of the best men that ever lived—Charles Kingsley:—

"I found myself forced to turn my back on race-courses, not because I did not love to see horses run—in that old English pleasure taken simply and alone I can fully sympathise—but because I found that they tempted me to betting, and that betting tempted me to company and to passions unworthy not merely of a scholar and a gentleman, but of an honest and rational bargeman or collier."

I feel a pride in being able to testify that I know of no poacher who bets. In fact, I do not believe that the thought of betting ever enters their minds. A standing wonder with them is how richer folk can breed and rear greyhounds and then sell them without hesitation when they fail to win money. The poacher-sportsman loves his dog as he does his child. There is not one among my acquaintances who would not be glad to see betting prohibited absolutely.

XXXIV

PILGRIMS OF THE NIGHT

THERE ARE MEN who travel all the way to the Rocky Mountains and to the jungles of Africa and India in order to enjoy sport. These are of the wealthy class, and many other men who are not so favoured by fortune envy them their opportunities. It does not appear to be known that there is no need to go so far away. In many parts of this country, and even in the neighbourhood of London, there is more game to the acre than in any of those distant parts, and the risk which must be run in order to take it depends altogether on the daring of the sportsman. The average poacher runs more risk and endures more punishment or suffering than the average hunter of the wolf or the wild boar.

There is no more enchanting pastime than that of walking in the country at night. An intimate acquaintance with every lane, footpath, and stile in West Kent and a large part of Surrey enables me to find my way there in the dark better than in daylight. A neighbourhood with which one becomes familiar in the night looks altogether different by day.

The men whose names are mentioned in these pages all agree that the one drawback of advancing years is that it deprives them of the power of enduring fatigue which is essential to the pilgrim of the night. There was a time when we could do the hardest day's work, and walk all night for sport, but we now begin to feel that we must find our happiness in the pleasures of the memory. It is said of old soldiers that in the warmth of the ale-house parlour they fight their battles afresh. In a very similar spirit have I penned these sketches. Thoughts of my brave and affectionate dogs can never fail to move me, and to recall exciting incidents of chase and combat quickens the pulse like a return to youth. A few words on my companions may be of interest.

Cardiff was born in the beautiful vale of Neath, near Swansea, and at a very early age was known to the neighbouring keepers. He had many tales to tell of an uncle who was a famous poacher, and who initiated him into the mysteries of the craft. The two were acquainted with every yard of the mountains which lie between Neath and Dowlais, and, indeed, their expeditions took them over a large part of Glamorganshire. Cardiff was apprenticed to the engineering trade, but matters became so hot that he was obliged to leave home before the term of his apprenticeship expired. He traversed a considerable part of England, and ultimately settled down in London. Gifted with a magnificent constitution, he hardly knew what fatigue meant. His whole heart was in the chase, and he imparted an element of humour to our proceedings which added greatly to their zest. He took an intense delight in fooling keepers, who are always yokels at bottom. He was continually placing himself in the most risky situations, and just as constantly extricated himself by means of his mother wit. Shaking hands with strange keepers and persuading them that he knew them when employed on another estate, was one of his favourite tricks. He was an intense lover of dogs, and often declared that if his means permitted he would keep a thousand. If a dog once entered his door it remained there for ever, as he could not bear to part with it. This often caused fluttering in the domestic dove-cot, which was a source of great amusement to his friends. He did not poach for profit, and only sold the proceeds of an expedition when the haul was so large that he did not know how to dispose of it otherwise. Sport for sport's own sake was the keynote of his career.

Coke was a man of another stamp. He was born on Salisbury Plain, and from infancy was familiar with dogs and hares. He had an abiding desire to become the owner, or failing that, the manager of a kennel of greyhounds. He reasoned, and quite correctly, that in order to achieve his object all that was necessary was to breed one first-rate greyhound. And so he bred litter after litter, but the dog he required never came. No matter how often he was disappointed, he was never disheartened, and always believed implicitly that the next litter would yield the specimen he sought. Every one acquainted with greyhound breeding knows that the mortality among puppies is very high, and Coke, in common with other breeders, always lost some from each litter. When he had reared and trained the remainder, and they disappointed his expectations, he was wont to console himself with the reflection that the dog that would have won died.

Although a genuine lover of sport, Coke was not such an enthusiast in the matter as Cardiff. His yard was constantly full of dogs, and he could not afford to keep on running them in coursing matches. He poached mainly because he did not know how to employ them otherwise. He was, however, an important addition to the gang, and knew all the tricks and retreats of every sort of game. He has not yet abandoned the hope of breeding a Master Magrath or a Fullerton. That his perseverance may be crowned with success is the earnest prayer of his old comrade.

Greenman was a carpenter by trade, and such an excellent mechanic that he was almost always made foreman by the employers he served. He, like the others, was a lover of sport and adventure, and in addition was a hater of landlords and aristocrats of all sorts. I believe he derived more pleasure from knowing, that he had deprived a landlord of a hare than from watching it coursed or putting it in his own pocket. He was inclined to be merciful towards keepers, whom he looked upon as tools and dupes, but I verily believe that if one of their masters crossed his path he would shoot him with as little compunction as he would a pheasant. A born rebel and law-breaker, he was yet the jolliest and most generous of companions, and left behind him an impression of kindliness and unselfishness which one could never forget.

Riverhead's history has already been indicated. He was brought up comfortably, and when, through no fault of his own, misfortunes came upon him he emerged from them like a man of courage. His ability and industry as a workman were acknowledged by all who knew him. He never had an employer who did not part from him with reluctance, and welcome him back when circumstances permitted. His energy was inexhaustible. He often, in addition to working in the daytime, had to work a night or even two nights a week, yet he was always willing to join the gang, and certainly no one was out more frequently. He was a true lover of sport and harmless fun of all sorts, kind-hearted and considerate, and never rough with keepers except when, as sometimes chanced, they assaulted his dogs. Like all of us he was a worshipper of his pets, and when Riverhead had to decide the question of man *versus* dog it always went hard with the man. Generous, steadfast, and incautious, he was the cause of my being fined over and over again. May all the acquaintances he makes be as harmless and unselfish as my old friend Sam.

Carlyle says that the Great Revolution was made by the poachers of France. The foregoing sketches will help the reader to understand the sort of men they were, and also, perhaps, to guess at those who would be likely to make their presence felt if troublous times arose in Britain.

AFTERWORD

... AND ALL THE TIME
A POACHER

J
AMES 'JIM' CONNELL was born on 27 March 1852 in McCormack's Yard, Rathniska, Kilskyre, Kells, County Meath, the eldest of thirteen children born to Thomas Connell and Ann Shaw, tenant farmers of Ballinlough Castle.[1] A gravestone in the old cemetery at Kilskyre gives his grandparents' names as Thomas and Jane Connell.[2] Some family members used O'Connell as their surname. A brother, Canon O'Connell, became a parish priest in Scarborough, Yorkshire, England,[3] and another brother was active in the Bridge Street Bakers' Society, forerunner of the Dublin No. 1 Branch, Irish Bakers', Confectioners' & Allied Workers' Amalgamated Union.[4]

EARLY LIFE AND JOHN LANDYE'S SOCIALIST TUTELAGE
Jim Connell's daughter, Norah Walshe, records that Thomas married Ann when she was nineteen years of age and that 'the schooling of farmers' children at that time was not the best', but that James got 'a few years' irregular schooling at the National School and helped on the farm'.[5] A regular duty minding sheep allowed Connell indulge his 'insatiable appetite for reading'. Depressed circumstances led the family to move to Birr, County Offaly (then King's County), where Thomas worked as a groom for the Earl of Rosse. Walshe remembers her grandfather, like her father, as having 'rather a wild, irresponsible nature' and imbuing his son with

a deep love of nature. Young James spent many days and nights rambling around the Slieve Blooms and Bog of Allen, acquiring his first taste of poaching, aided and abetted by his friend Brennan from the Royal Irish Constabulary (RIC), who taught him some of the poacher's wiles—how to dam trout streams and snare wild geese. [6] The youngster developed a love of poetry, which he wrote to reflect the bucolic idyll he roamed through. Thomas passed on a great knowledge of horses to his son and thirty years later James published *The Horse and How to Treat Him* (London, nd). Books were plentiful and varied in Birr and young Connell must have been impressed by Rosse's interest in astronomy and his construction of the world's largest telescope.[7] It was in Birr that Connell said he was first sworn into the Republican Brotherhood, the Fenians, in 1870, claiming to have repeated this oath in London in 1875.

In 1867, the Connell family moved to Dublin. Ann Connell wished for her eldest son to enter the priesthood but the nearest he got was some general labouring work at St Patrick's College, Maynooth. Connell rejected Catholicism at an early age, his interests being political rather than religious, although he developed a fascination with evolution, theosophy and Buddhism.[8] One of Connell's most famous public talks was a discourse 'From protoplasm to man' that Francis Williams recalls as being so erudite 'he was never known in the course of a two hours' talk to get beyond the introduction'.[9] Dublin's developing socialist circle soon attracted Connell and he fell under the influence of John Landye, a fellow Meath man, debating theoretical matters on Sunday rambles with the Free Literary Union.[10] Landye had been active in the International Working Men's Association and, as a 'veteran Internationalist', was still speaking on socialist themes in Dublin in the late 1880s.[11] Here he met, among others, Fred Ryan, a pioneer socialist and later the Secretary of Cummancht na hÉireann/ Socialist Party of Ireland.[12] Norah Walshe recognized Landye's immense impact on her father:

Under the tuition of Landye the seeds of Socialism were sown and soon Connell became a fluent and attractive speaker and debater. Landye's method was to conduct every Sunday a group of young, intelligent men in free discussion about everything under the sun. They tramped the hills and mountains with their leader, exhilarated in mind and body. My father loved Landye to the end of his life and there is no doubt his early influence fired the adolescent enthusiasm of Connell into lasting flame. [13]

Connell must have been in his element. Sometimes Landye would be asked questions he could not answer and withhold discussion until the following week.

He seemed to be able to absorb knowledge from some inner source of consciousness as well as outward enquiry. He was truly a remarkable man if all my father told me about him was true. He too had had scarcely any education and actually taught himself to read and write when he was turned twenty and then his progress was so rapid that he soon outshone many well-educated people by natural ability, and they were glad to listen to him with reverence and respect. My father was indeed lucky to have found him at that time.

Another friend of the Connell family thought that Landye sounded like a 'peripatetic Irish Socrates'. [14]

Connell was employed as a docker and became party to an unsuccessful attempt to organize the casual workforce. Although providing an exciting education, Dublin 'eventually proved disappointing' for Connell. [15] He brought his thirst and enthusiasm for socialism, built upon an already developed sense of Irish self-determination, with him when he migrated to London in 1875, to seek work, having been blacked on the Dublin docks.

LONDON, LAND LEAGUE & SOCIAL DEMOCRATIC FEDERATION

Connell quickly continued his political involvement, claiming to have founded the first London branch of the National Land

League of Great Britain (NLLGB) in Poplar in 1879 and served on its executive.[16] The NLLGB was, in fact, inaugurated on 25 March 1881, under the presidency of Justin McCarthy. On 1 February 1881, Michael Davitt had urged on Parnell a 'junction' between Irish nationalism and British democracy. The most tangible result was the formation of the NLLGB intended to inform British workers about the Irish Land Question and 'their community of interests' with Irish tenant farmers.[17] H.M. Hyndman of the Democratic Federation, which was set up in June 1881 partly to oppose British coercion in Ireland and which became the Social Democratic Federation (SDF) in 1883, served on the NLLGB Executive.[18]

Connell claimed original membership of the SDF, remaining active for ten years although he 'never cared for the management'.[19] He certainly associated with Hyndman and wrote regularly for the SDF organ, *Justice*. In September 1890 he became SDF candidate in Finchley East and was immediately attacked by the Liberal candidate, James Rowlands, and T.P. O'Connor, owner of the *Star*, who feared that the constituency's considerable Irish vote would be lost to the Conservatives and Unionists.[20] On 20 September 1890 *Justice* reported that SDF members 'have been treated to brutal and cowardly treatment at the hands of the Irish and Liberals'. At a large meeting held in the Hall of Science, Connell 'went pluckily through his address' despite being 'saluted by filthy and blackguardly expressions, one ruffian going so far as to kick Comrade Connell'. Asked if he would retire in the event of a vote of no confidence, Connell

> seized the red flag and waived it above his head, amid the most loud and prolonged cheering of the meeting, saying that in spite of the paid bullies, if they did not kill him in the attempt, he would continue to carry aloft the red flag. And in the event of the workers of East Finchley returning him to Parliament ... he would raise the red flag in the House of Commons.[21]

The 'red flag' episode was used in an inverted way as a 'red scare' among Catholic, Irish voters whom, in an era of *rerum novarum*, were encouraged to think of socialists as 'crafty agitators', atheists, proponents of free love and the expropriators of private property.[22] Connell nevertheless flew the red flag at all his meetings, although he did not ultimately contest the election.[23]

Later, he became active in the Independent Labour Party (ILP). In 1888, he was named in *The Times*-Parnell Commission on Parnellism and Crime as an 'advocate of treason, sedition, assassination and violence'.[24] His daughter felt that Fenianism 'did not interest him for long' but in the 1898 *Labour Annual* he was still listed as being a 'member of a Fenian organization'. By the time he wrote 'The Red Flag', as he put it, 'he had shaken Fenianism off'.[25]

SPEAKER, PAMPHLETEER AND POET

Connell's source of income is unclear—other than from the fruits of his poaching. In the *Labour Yearbook* he is listed as a speaker on 'socialism, Darwinism, philosophy and the game laws', [26] From 1909 until his death he was Secretary of the Workingmen's Legal Aid Society based in Chancery Lane, Fleet Street, London, providing advice on compensation and other claims.[27] He was well known in Fleet Street, being visited in his favourite haunt—the Golden Cross in the Strand—by many contemporary figures. He was six feet one inch tall, wore a black sombrero, flowing Inverness cape and bright red scarf, and his theatrical manner led many to think of him as a Shakespearian actor. [28] Walshe adds that his tie was 'sometimes green for Ireland'.[29] He undertook speaking tours, spending much time away from his family home. He visited Scotland regularly and became 'very friendly with the Astronomer Royal in Edinburgh', spending 'hours in the observatory, looking through the giant telescope and he made himself very familiar with astronomy'.[30] Such a lifestyle put great strain on his family. In 1882 Connell had married Catherine Aungier, an Englishwomen, but lack of money put stress on the relationship.[31]

Katherine Gatty, one of a number of lodgers in the family home in Denmark Hill, recalls the Connells' precarious circumstances:

> We all paid Kitty Connell a good deal over the actual value of our rooms, and, besides this, when there was a threat, the gas being cut off or the bailiffs coming in, we would all contribute to a whip round to extricate the Connells temporarily. We all felt that the extra rent was worth it, for the sake of other advantages, not least of these the stream of Jim's monologues in the sort of vocabulary afterwards familiarised by Lady Gregory's plays, flowing freely in that melodious Meath brogue, scintillating with delicious humour.[32]

In 1962 Norah Walshe told Andrew Boyd that she was the 'only remaining child of that marriage' and that her mother too had the 'pioneer temperament and she hoped great things of her husband and urged him to further [political] work'.[33] 'Marriage and a few years prosperity' initially developed Connell 'into a very striking personality', if 'inclined to stoutness'. Connell and Aungier 'separated for good' when Norah Walshe was thirteen years old as he was 'impossible to live with for long, his personality was too overpowering'. She went to live with her mother but 'always kept in touch with my father for the rest of his life'.

'THE RED FLAG'

Connell published a successful series of pamphlets, among them *Brothers at Last – A Centenary Appeal to Celt and Saxon* (London and Glasgow, 1898); and *Glasgow Municipal Enterprises* (Glasgow, 1897). In the first, he argued that the Independent Labour Party was the alternative to British Toryism and Liberalism and Irish, bourgeois nationalism'.[34] In *Socialism and the Survival of the Fittest*, (London, 1897) he applied his observations of wildlife to socialist theory, pointing to the natural communism of ants, beavers and bees. His reading was reflected in extensive quotations from contemporary sociologists and scientists such as Herbert Spencer and John

Tyndall.[35] In the 21 December 1889 edition of *Justice*, under the heading 'A Christmas Carol', Harry Quelch published Connell's anthem 'The Red Flag'. It appeared on a Thursday and by Saturday was being sung in Liverpool and Glasgow. Connell had earlier written similar songs—'The Workers of England' and 'The Workers of Ireland', the latter appearing in *The Socialist Song Book*.[36] He claimed that 'The Red Flag' was written on a fifteen-minute train journey from Charing Cross to New Cross and was intended to raise morale during the Great London Dock Strike. [37] However, Katherine Gatty's recollection differs from Connell's explanation.

> Keir Hardie had come to Denmark Hill one Friday evening to chose a kitten and, in the kitchen, with his back to a fire that would have roasted an ox, Jim told us how he came to compose 'The Red Flag'. He said it was after closing and he was walking home over Blackfriars Bridge, talking to friends of the docker's tanner fight and then he went on alone, and the air from the Thames rose to cool his forehead, and as it blew he felt inside his brain the words of the poem crowding into it so fast, he feared by the morn's morn they be all forgot. So he took out a pen and wrote them as soon as he had the door open. [38]

The song was inspired by Connell's knowledge of and commitment to international class struggle. In his 1920 explanation, he talks of the Land League, the London Dockers—who 'day after day … marched with their red rags on poles'—and the New Unionism, Rand miners and Russian Nihilists, 'the parents of the Bolsheviks'.[39]

> It was my privilege to know Stepniak, himself one of the greatest Terrorists. I was in his company the night he was accidentally killed at a level crossing on a railway. His book *Underground Russia*, produced a greater effect on me than any 'revelation' ever produced on a devotee.[40]

Connell felt he was indeed 'raised above myself' by the daunt-
less courage of Vera Sassulitch and the 'endless abnegation' of
Sophia Pervoskaya', two notorious revolutionary Russians.[41] He
also referred to the 1887 hanging of Chicago's Haymarket martyrs
and how he heard one of their widows, Mrs Lucy Parsons, say
that 'she was glad her husband had died as he did'.[42] All this, he
thought, might help the reader 'understand how the souls of all
true Socialists were elevated and how I got into the mood which
enabled me to write "The Red Flag"', Connell was perhaps 'trig-
gered' to write the song after attending an SDF meeting where
Herbert Burrows had described socialism as his religion.[43]

Although Connell makes no reference to it, 'The Red Flag' by
the Chartist poet, Alfred Fennell, first published in *Red Republican*,
1850, may have proved his inspiration.[44] A further influence could
have been Gerald Massey's 'The Red Flag' from *Song of the Red
Republican*, 1850.[45] Connell wrote 'his poem' to be sung to the popular Jacobite air, 'The White Cockade' but in 1895 Adolphe
Smythe Headingley rearranged it for the tune 'Maryland' or 'Die
Tannenbaum', to which most people still sing it. George Bernard
Shaw dismissed the new tune as sounding like a 'funeral dirge to
eels'.[46] Connell hated the new air:

> It is Church music and was, no doubt, composed, and is cer-
> tainly calculated, to remind people of their sins, and frighten
> them into repentance. I dare say it is very good music for the
> purpose for which it was composed, but that purpose was wide-
> ly different from mine ...[47]

'The White Cockade' was the one 'known to everyone in Ireland
fifty years ago', not the version 'on sale in music shops today' as
'some fool has altered it by introducing minor notes into it, until
it is now nearly a jig'.[48] On hearing it sung to 'Die Tannenbaum'
at the conclusion of a 1925 Labour Party Conference, Connell
'could do nothing but say over again, with deep reproach, "Ye
sp'iled me pome! Ye sp'iled me pome."[49]

The people's flag is deepest red,
It shrouded oft our martyred dead,
And, ere their limbs grew stiff and cold
Their hearts' blood died its every fold.
Then raise the scarlet standard high.
Though cowards flinch and traitors sneer.
We'll keep the Red Flag flying here.

Labour Party leader, James Ramsay MacDonald liked neither the song nor its author. In 1925 Henry Hamilton Fyfe, editor of the *Daily Herald*, organized a competition with a £50 prize to find a new, better Labour anthem. Fyfe, whilst acknowledging that no one 'could fail to be stirred by it', thought it too often 'badly sung, often dragged and slurred', and there are 'many who agree with Mr MacDonald in wishing for some other Labour song to be the anthem of the Movement'.[50] Judges were Hugh Roberton, conductor of the Glasgow Orpheus Choir, and, incongruously perhaps, the Irish tenor, John McCormack. Over three hundred earnest entries all received 'careful attention' but failed to produce a winner. Fyfe said that 'The Red Flag' would 'remain in possession of the field'. Walshe recalls that her father, then 'getting very feeble, waited with tears in his eyes for the result'. It would 'have broken his heart to see his song displaced. After the result he received hundreds of letters of congratulations. We were very glad'.[51] In 1934 Jim Middleton, the TUC General Secretary, had wondered did the song belong to 'an older time', was it 'anachronistic in a more educated, a freer, a more sophisticated age?' Surveying continuing struggle, however, he concluded that the song still had merit as 'freedom's fight is not yet won'.[52] 'The Red Flag' continued to be sung at the conclusion of Labour Party conferences and raised the rafters of the House of Commons when it was sung by 393 victorious Labour MPs after the 1945 general election. It has been a standard in socialist songbooks internationally since it first appeared. [53]

Connell wrote scores of verses, many published in the Left press. He was a staff member of Keir Hardie's *Labour Leader*. Irish labour papers also published his works— 'The Blackleg' appeared in the *Irish Worker* on 22 November 1913 and 'The Miner' was printed in *Voice of Labour* on 16 August 1918. A collection, *Red Flag Rhymes*, was published by the Agitator's Press, Huddersfield, and *Labour Leader*, Glasgow 1900, and was republished in several editions. 'The Miners' Song' is typical of his agitational verse and is remarkable as it was written long before the South Wales Miners' Federation became the first group to demand nationalization of the pits in 1911.[54]

> Deep in the gloom of the great earth's womb
> We force the birth of coal;
> The power that moves the nation's wheels,
> To the furnace fires we roll;
> We dig out wealth at the cost of health
> To gild Oppression's shrine; .
> 'Twil aye be so,
> For a wage of woe,
> Till the miners own the mine.

Salvation comes in the final verse where

> We'll drive despair from the bright'ning air,
> And hands and hearts combine;
> And we'll find our health
> In the Commonwealth,
> When the miners own the mine.

This was a common theme, as in his poem 'The Village and the Mill', first published in *Justice*, June 1889,

> The people seized and worked the mill
> And when the goods were sold
> The price was fairly portioned out
> Among the young and old.

... AND ALL THE WHILE A POACHER

In *Labour's Who's Who,* Connell listed 'poaching' as his recreation.[55] From London, he rambled in the Surrey hills and Kent marshes with a number of constant companions, poaching pheasants, partridges, hares and rabbits. He was caught on a number of occasions and fined, although he found sympathy for his trade among both magistrates and police that he appeared before.[56] He expressed his contempt for the game laws in verse,

> In boyhood I quaffed with a passionate love,
> The breath of the mountain and moor,
> And hated the greed of the covetous lord
> Who fenced out the weak and the poor;
> And later, through covert and pheasant stocked glade
> I swept like a blast of the north,
> I broke ev'ry law the land robbers made
> And mocked at the strength they put forth.[57]

The Humanitarian League published his *The Truth About the Game Laws: A Record of Cruelty, Selfishness and Oppression,* (1898), although not 'caring for his views on poaching and trapping animals'.[58] His biggest seller was *Confessions of a Poacher,* published by Arthur Pearson in 1901, 80,000 copies being sold in two editions.[59] Walshe thought her father 'very inconsistent all his life', sometimes displaying 'the wild uncontrolled impulses of primitive country-born nature, free and untrammelled' and at others 'he was keenly intellectual'. In *Confessions,* she thought 'a psychologist can see the dual nature of the man'.[60]

> Personally I think it is a cruel book and always wish the subject had been a healthier one. I think Socialism should include all animals under its protection and nothing should be hunted for mass pleasure by the proletariat. I used to tell my father that but he did not want to see my point of view. All the same, he could be very kind to animals sometimes and would stop people in the street ill-treating horses. [61]

Confessions portrays much cruelty, with birds and hares being coursed, snared, trapped, shot, blinded by birdlime or gassed by sulphurous candles. It also displays Connell's physical courage or bravado when confronted by or involved in altercations with keepers; and his passion for and understanding of dogs, particularly lurchers, especially his two favourites, Nellie and Blucher. In *Red Flag Rhymes*, he wrote of 'My Nellie':

> Let me sing about my Nellie
> Just for moments one or two,
> Let me tell about her goodness
> And the deeds that she can do.
> She's the fondest friend I number,
> She's the leader of the chase,
> She's the queen of all the poachers,
> And the bravest of her race.

Connell appeared most complete and relaxed in the company of his hounds. He expressed regrets about some poaching techniques but *Confessions* is an unapologetic book, at odds with current Labour movement revulsion of blood sports. Connell derived some income from poaching but 'he would give away his hares generously' and seems to have been rewarded more by the thrill, adventure and the contribution to his notoriety.[62] Gatty recalls that Connell's wife 'would be in an agony of anxiety till he returned' from his regular poaching trips and that she 'used to shudder at his bag next day'.[63]

DEATH, OBSCURITY AND COMMEMORATION

Connell became an obscure figure after his death.[64] Though his anthem lived on, few had any idea who had written it.[65] Labour historian Andrew Boyd began to uncover the mystery of Connell's life.[66] It led to a 1962 BBC radio broadcast, 'The Man who Wrote "The Red Flag"'. New information came from listeners in response.[67] In 1975, Tommy Grimes, then a baker member of Kells Trades Council, who knew 'The Red Flag' was written by a 'man who came from County Meath', learned that Connell was born 'down the road in Kilskyre'.[68] Grimes discovered from a Minute Book of the Ballinlough Back to the Land Committee that Connell had addressed a gathering in Crossakiel in 1918, his last known visit to Ireland before his death.[69] After much fund-raising and annual seminars, the Jim Connell Memorial Committee unveiled a monument at the crossroads in Crossakiel on 26 April 1998. The ceremony was performed by Peter Cassells, General Secretary, ICTU, a Navan man, and Mary Turner, President of the British Union GMB, originally from Thurles, County Tipperary.[70] Considerable assistance was received from Lewisham where the Council had unveiled a plaque on Connell's home on his sixtieth anniversary in 1989.[71]

Connell had died in Lewisham Hospital, South London, on 8 February 1929, after a seizure. He was cremated on 14 February 1929, 'a bitterly cold day', at Golder's Green Crematorium. Veteran Labour leader Tom Mann conducted the secular proceedings and the assembly were addressed by George Hicks, General Secretary, Building Workers' Trade Union, representing the TUC General Council; William O'Brien, General Secretary, Irish Transport and General Workers' Union; and Shapurji Saklatvala, Communist MP for Battersea.[72]

It is hard to assess Connell. A 'loveable rogue' and 'great character' undoubtedly, but a minor figure at the fringe of the British Labour movement. Gatty reflects that he 'mixed in the best society in England', knowing Annie Beasant, Edward Bellamy, R.B. Cunningham Grahame, Walter Crane, Pete Curran, Henry George, Keir Hardie, Jean Jaures, Karl Liebknecht, Tom Mann, William Morris, Philip Snowden, Stepniak, Klara Zetkin and any number of 'Irish MPs', all of whom 'were glad to go out and see Jim and to meet his friends at Denmark Hill'.[73] But their concern for Connell's company surely went beyond mere amusement at his eccentricity and tall tales: Gatty offers a dismissive assessment.

Though he was so typically the 'stage Irishman', Jim Connell was not among Ireland's great emancipators or poets, the Celtic Renaissance owes him nothing. His Fenianism, his Socialism and his Theosophy, I think, were nebulous.

But beyond that, she suddenly captures the point, intended or otherwise, of Connell's life:

But, like Rouget de Lisle with 'La Marseillaise', he wrote a song that has become famous, that has inspired thousands, and that can never die. He was never a Communist, but for writing 'The Red Flag', Lenin sent him the Order of the Soviet Star.[74]

After Connell's death, Walshe gave this medal to Tom Mann 'by request'. Mann, at the crematorium, said Connell was 'no meek and mild platitudinarian. He was first and foremost a fighter. "The Red Flag" had inspired thousands, possibly millions'. A red flag draped his coffin with the hopeful words 'Socialism Advances' inscribed upon it.[75] James Connolly wrote:

No revolutionary movement is complete without its poetical expression. If such a movement has caught hold of the imagination of the masses, they will seek a vent in song for the aspirations, the fears and hopes, the loves and hatreds engendered by the struggle. Until the movement is marked by the joyous, defiant singing of revolutionary songs, it lacks one of the distinctive marks of a popular revolutionary movement: it is the dogma of a few, not the faith of the multitude. [76]

Connell's daughter, Norah, concluded her memoir, 'because I have written this little sketch of my father's life it must not be thought that I overrated his work'. She acknowledged others had 'done as much and more that he did for Socialism in a long lifetime'. She recognized that his 'poetical and literary ability was not of the highest order' and that 'a little' of his personality 'went a long way', that at home he could be 'autocratic, dogmatic and over-bearing' and that he carried a 'touch of mysticism'. He was a 'loyal friend' but a 'bitter enemy'.[77] Privately, she conceded that, in later years, he may have been 'over fond of drink'. All this notwithstanding, Walshe clearly loved and respected her father, admired his achievements and derived huge pride in his writing 'The Red Flag'.

The *Daily Herald* noted that he was 'essentially a man of the people' and that he described himself as a 'sheep farmer, dock labourer, navvy, railwayman, draper, lawyer of a sort and all the time a poacher'.[78] On the commonage at Crossakiel, where the Connell Monument now stands, visitors can read his 'Old Poacher's Song',[79] feel the wind, smell the blossoms, hay or grass, and gaze across drumlin hills stretching north into Cavan, and wander freely with the spirit they have encountered and maybe rise a hare or two!

> Oh, grant me an ownerless corner of earth,
> Or pick me a hillock of stones,
> Or gather the wind-wafted leaves of the trees
> To cover my socialist bones,
> Though small is the debt that humanity owes
> To this shrunken remainder of me,
> Yet, yet I deserve that my litter at last
> From the taint of the thief shall be free.

FRANCIS DEVINE
SIPTU College, Dublin, October 2004

NOTES

1. This essay is an expanded version of an entry on Connell in the 2004 *Oxford Dictionary of National Biography*.

2. The headstone is illustrated in 'The Jim Connell story: From Cross-akiel to sing Labour's struggle' in *Jim Connell: Author of 'The Red Flag': Memorial Unveiling, 26 April, 1998* (Kells, 1998) p. 7. The stone names the place as Kilskeer. There is also a photograph of the original flags of the Connell homestead still extant in McCormack's Yard.

3. Andrew Boyd, *Jim Connell: Author of 'The Red Flag'* (Belfast, 2001) p. 13. He apparently prayed for Connell on a weekly basis such was his concern for his wayward brother's path.

4. John P. Swift, *John Swift: An Irish Dissident* (Dublin, 1991) p. 36. John Swift, 1896–1990, the bakers' leader was imprisoned in Wormwood Scrubs in 1917 as a conscientious objector and first heard an inmate whistling 'The Red Flag' as the prisoners learned of the Bolshevik Revolution. At that time he was unfamiliar with the song.

5. Andrew Boyd, Francis Devine and Tommy Grimes, 'Norah Walshe and the rescue of Jim Connell', *Saothar* 24, 1999, pp. 91–9, reproduces in full Walshe's manuscript, *James Connell: A Biographical Sketch by his Daughter, Norah Walshe*, which was originally sent to Andrew Boyd in February 1962 after she heard his radio broadcast on 27 January 1962, 'The Man who Wrote "The Red Flag"'. Walshe's view contrasts with Connell's claim that his education was a 'few weeks under a hedge' and that he learned 'little more than reading and writing'. That his education was fitful and interrupted is probably true, however.

6. James Connell, *Confessions of a Poacher* (London, 1901) Chapter II, 'Early Days'.

7. William Parsons, Third Earl of Rosse, 1800–67, constructed the world's then largest telescope between 1839–45, using local craftsmen and much invention.

8. His 'bible' in such matters was A.P. Sinnett, *Esoteric Buddhism* (London, 1883).

9. Francis Williams, *Fifty Years March: The Rise of the Labour Party* (London, nd), p. 103.

10. William O'Brien, *Forth The Banners Go* (Dublin, 1969) p. 17. Landye was from Kilmessan.

11. John W. Boyle, *The Irish Labour Movement in the Nineteenth Century* (Washington, 1988) pp. 172–7. He addressed the Progressist Club on 'What do we mean by progress?' in May 1889.

12. Fred Ryan, 1874–1913, a member of the Irish Socialist Republican Party, 1896; first Secretary, Socialist Party of Ireland, 1909; and first Secretary, Abbey Theatre. See Manus O'Riordan (ed.), *Socialism, Democracy and the Church* (Dublin, 1984).

13. Walshe, *op. cit.* p. 95.

14. Francis Devine, 'Katherine Gatty's memories of Jim Connell in *Labour News*', article in preparation for *Saothar*. Her recollections appeared in *Labour News*, 26 December 1936, a Dublin Labour Party paper. She was a veteran suffragette and had lodged with the Connell family in Denmark Hill. The full quotation is 'Landye, an entirely self-taught philosopher, would, like a peripatetic Irish Socrates, gather about him a group of intelligent and inquiring proletarian youths, with whom he would discuss all the problems of the universe during interminable tramps through the Wicklow Mountains or on long winter evenings in some small crowded Dublin "pub".' It was Gatty who first edited and published Norah Walshe's memoir.

15. The comment on Dublin is Walshe's observation. The Dublin Quay Labourers' Union with 1500 members was conspicuous in the 1875 O'Connell centenary celebrations.

16. T.W. Moody, *Davitt and the Irish Revolution, 1846–1882* (Oxford, 1981) p. 481.

17. It has been claimed that Connell was involved in Michael Davitt's Irish Democratic Trade & Labour Federation, formed in Cork on 21 January 1891 'to reassert the claims of labour within the national movement'. This seems unlikely as the organization does not appear to have operated much outside of Munster and not at all in Britain, see Emmet O'Connor, *A Labour History of Ireland, 1824–1960*

(Dublin, 1992) pp. 52–3 and Moody, *op. cit.* p. 548.

18. H.M. Hyndman, *Record of an Adventurous Life* (London, 1911) pp. 255–7 and Fintan Lane, *The Origins of Modern Irish Socialism, 1881–1896* (Cork, 1997) pp. 32 ff. Henry Myers Hyndman, 1842–1921, was born into a prosperous family and graduated from Trinity College, Cambridge, studied for the bar and travelled widely. After reading *Das Kapital*, he converted to Socialism and founded the Democratic Federation in 1881. He published *The Historical Basis for Socialism*, 1883, and led the SDF, only for his authoritarian manner and inflexibility to cause splits. He became a believer in the Parliamentary road and supported the Allied cause in the First World War, against the belief of most socialists.

19. Walshe, *op. cit.* p. 95.

20. C.D. Greaves, *The Life and Times of James Connolly* (London, 1961) p. 49.

21. Cited in Boyd, *Jim Connell, op. cit.* p. 23.

22. Pope Leo XIII's anti-socialist encyclical was issued in 1891.

23. Martin Crick, *The History of the Social Democratic Federation* (Keele, 1994) 'Appendix C: SDF/BSP/NSP Parliamentary Election Results, 1885–1924', pp. 329–31.

24. Andrew Boyd, *The Rise of the Irish Trade Unions, 1729–1970* (Tralee, 1972) p. 58.

25. Boyd, *Jim Connell, op. cit.* p. 17.

26. *Labour Year Book*, various editions 1890s.

27. John Monks, then General Secretary, TUC, explained that in a 'pre-Welfare State era, this voluntary society helped injured workers to make claims against their employers', 'Freedom's fight … not yet won', *Jim Connell: Author of 'The Red Flag', op. cit.* p. 14.

28. Boyd, *Jim Connell, op. cit.* pp. 31–2 received this information from Wal Hannington.

29. Walshe, *op. cit.* p. 97. This was always so on St Patrick's Day!

30. *Ibid.* Indication perhaps of his Birr experience resurfacing!

31. Nothing is known of Aungier or what became of her after the separation. Walshe suggests her mother also had the (political) 'pioneer spirit', suggesting a progressive attitude.

32. Gatty, *op. cit.* The other lodgers were Frank Penny and Fred Pickles, like the young journalist Gatty, part of the *Clarion* office team with Keir Hardie.

33. Walshe, *op. cit.* p. 97. There is no record of any other Connell children.

34. Boyd, *Jim Connell, op. cit.* p. 24. The Glasgow pamphlet champions 'gas and water socialism', the city's municipal socialism being lauded.
35. *Ibid.* p. 20.
36. 'Workers of England' appeared in *Chants for Labour* edited by Edward Carpenter in 1888, illustrated by Walter Crane. Both were to be sung to *O'Donnell Abú*. Carpenter, 1844–1929, graduated from Cambridge and became a vicar in 1870. He left the Church in 1874, joined the SDF in 1883 and ILP in 1893. He is most famous for a series of pamphlets championing sexual freedom. Crane, 1845–1915, was an apprentice engraver to Linton, an old Chartist; a Liberal he campaigned for the Reform Act, 1867; met William Morris in 1870 and joined the SDF, illustrating *Justice*; joined Socialist League, 1888, work in *Commonwealth*; later in Fabian Society and Labour Party; head, Royal College of Art but resigned; celebrated engraver and illustrator.
37. Jim Connell, 'How I wrote "The Red Flag"', *The Call*, 6 May 1920. A widely held belief, no doubt based on Connell's own account, was that he had written it whilst travelling by train from Glasgow to London. For an account of the strike for 'the full orb of the docker's tanner' see Terry McCarthy, *The Great Dock Strike 1889* (London, 1988) and Ken Coates and Tony Topham, *The History of The Transport and General Workers' Union, Vol. 1, Part 1, 1870–1911: From Forerunners to Federation* (Oxford, 1991) pp. 54–73, 95–6, 117, 131, 246.
38. Gatty, *op. cit.*
39. John Gorman, *Banner Bright: An Illustrated History of Trade Union Banners* (London, 1986) p. 20.
40. Connell, *The Call, op. cit.* Sergius Mikhailovich Kravchinsky, 1832–95, fled Russia in 1878 after taking part in the assassination of the Czarist Chief of Police. *Underground Russia*, written in Italian in 1882 and translated into English in 1888, profiled Russian revolutionaries. His novel, *The Career of a Nihilist* or *Andrei Kozhukhov* (1889) was critically acclaimed by Shaw. He was killed in Turnham Green in 1895. In London circles he was known as Stepniak. E. Belfort Bax described him as 'of powerful build, thickset and of strong Mongoloid face and figure', a 'prominent personality in advanced London society during the eighties and nineties', *Reminiscences and Reflections of a Mid and Late Victorian* (London, 1918).
41. Vera Sassulitch, born in 1851, denied her privileged background and was acquitted after being tried for shooting General Trepoff, the

Czarist Chief of Police. Sophia Perovskaya, 1851–81, was the daughter of the Governor-General of St Petersburg, joined Land & Liberty group and then People's Will. She was hung for her part in the assassination attempt on Czar Alexander II.

42. Lucy E. Parsons, 1853–1942, was of black, native American and Mexican stock; dressmaker; strongly political and a campaigner for free speech, her husband Albert was one of the Haymarket victims; she remained politically active all her life. See her *To Tramps: The Unemployed, the Disinherited and Miserable* (Chicago, 1884); and Carolyn Ashbaugh, *Lucy Parsons* (Chicago, 1976); and Caeli Thibeault, *Lucy Parsons: A Life Dedicated to Justice* (Carbondale, 1998). Modern May Day grew out of the Chicago protests against the killing of alleged anarchist bombers, one of whom was Albert Parsons.

43. Monks, *Jim Connell: Author of 'The Red Flag'*, op. cit. Herbert Burrows, 1845–1921, a founder member, SDF; long-time friend of Annie Beasant, supporting her during the Match Girls' Strike, 1888; active in the London Dock Strike, 1889; with her turned to theosophy. Crick, *op. cit.* suggests that the song's 'sneering traitors' may well have been enemies within the fractious SDF, p. 77. 'Labour fakirs' were certainly in Connell's mind but they were surely not confined to the SDF.

44. J.W. Kovalyov, *An Anthology of Chartist Literature* (Moscow, 1956). This point is made by John McDonnell, *Songs of Struggle and Protest* (Dublin, 1979; Cork and Dublin, 1986).

45. Edmund and Ruth Frow, *Radical and Red Poets and Poetry* (Manchester, 1994) p. 59. Massey, 1828–1907, was a Chartist, Christian Socialist, poet and mystic. In 1849 he edited the Chartist paper *The Spirit of Freedom* where this verse first appeared.

46. Hannington to Andrew Boyd, 12 April 1960.

47. Connell, *The Call*, op. cit.

48. The Jacobites wore no uniform as such put placed a white cockade in their blue bonnets.

49. 'White Cockade, Tannenbaum or Maryland?' in *Jim Connell: Author of 'The Red Flag'*, op. cit. p. 16.

50. Cited in Boyd, *Jim Connell*, op. cit. and p. 33.

51. *Ibid.* The air to 'The White Cockade' is reproduced on p. 17.

52. Middleton's comments were in a foreword to a TUC songbook as part of the Tolpuddle Martyrs Centenary in 1934

53. It was printed in the *Industrial Bulletin*, 25 July 1908, journal of the

Industrial Workers of the World (IWW) in America and in versions of their *IWW Song Book* ever since.

54. *The Miners' Next Step* was published in 1911 by the Mid Rhondda Unofficial Reform Committee and is regarded as a classic, syndicalist document, see Hywel Francis and Dai Smith, *The Fed: A History of the South Wales Miners in the Twentieth Century* (London, 1980) pp. 10–13, 16, 186–7, 419, 444.

55. *Labour's Who's Who* (London, 1927).

56. Connell was fined £1 with 13s. 6d. costs at Croydon Magistrates and again at Woolwich Police Court. On both occasions Connell claimed a magistrate and a police inspector approached him after the case to seek supplies of game, see *Confessions of a Poacher* and Boyd, *Jim Connell, op. cit.* p. 15.

57. *Red Flag Rhymes*; and Boyd, *Jim Connell, op. cit.* p. 14. ff. Walshe, *op. cit.* p. 96.

58. Walshe, *op. cit.* p. 96.

59. It had first been serialized in *Titbits*. Although not reproduced in this edition, the original was illustrated by S.T. (Stephen) Dadd, 1879–1914, figure painter and illustrator contributing domestic and animal subjects to *The Graphic, Illustrated London News* and *The Rambler*, exhibiting widely; see Simon Houfe, *The Dictionary of 19th Century British Book Illustrators & Caricaturists* (Woodbridge, 1966) p. 111.

60. Walshe, *op. cit.* p. 97.

61. *Ibid.* p. 98.

62. Gatty, *op. cit.*

63. *Ibid.*

64. Even before his death, Connell becomes hard to trace. It is not known precisely what his attitude to the First World War was, although he would have shared initial socialist opposition to the conflict, nor even the Easter Rising. His support for the Rising and indeed Irish self-determination may be guessed, however, particularly from his scathing attack on 'dirty little Tim' Healy who did 'his master's menial work' and 'fed and fattened on the fare his benefactor spread'. Connell said he would buy a tomahawk and join the Red Indians if Healy ever governed Ireland but in 1922, when Healy was appointed Governor-General, he was maybe too old to carry out his threat! See Boyd, *Jim Connell, op. cit.* pp. 27–29.

65. Frank Edwards, Waterford International Brigader, thought Connell an 'Ulsterman' and that the tune was the *Green Cockade*. John Swift,

Bakers' Union leader, imagined him a 'Cavan man', see Uinseann MacEoin, *Survivors* (Dublin, 1980) pp. 15, 67.

66. Devine, 'Andrew Boyd and the rescue of Jim Connell', *op. cit.* and Boyd, *Jim Connell, op. cit.* pp. 39–45, 'Finding Jim Connell'.

67. BBC Home Service, Saturday, 27 January 1962.

68. *Jim Connell: Author of 'The Red Flag', op. cit.* p. 3. Tommy had heard the song sung by local man Kevin Smith. The occasion was a talk by Francis Devine for the Irish Labour History Society.

69. The minute book is signed 'P. Gaughran, Secretary, 1920' and was given to Grimes by Gaughran's daughter, Mary Mulvany. Connell had been an 'adviser' to the Committee and 'under his guidance they achieved some success' in acquiring lands from landlords in Ballyhist, Belview, Clonabraney, Deerpark, Distantrath, Kingsmountain and Rahand, *Jim Connell: 150th Anniversary, 1852–2002* (Kells, 2002) p. 17.

70. The sculptor was Michael Keane, Trim. Images of it can be seen in Boyd, Devine and Grimes, *op. cit.* in the various commemorative pamphlets issued in Kells; and, together with detailed information and colour images of Connell and the Kells celebrations, on http://www.dcu.ie/~comms/hsheehan/connell.htm

71. Boyd, Devine and Grimes, *op. cit.* p. 93. The plaque at 22A Stonton Park, Forest Hill Gate, London was unveiled by Gordon Brown, MP on 14 February 1989. This prompted the involvement in the Kells project of the GMB, London Region; Battersea & Wandsworth Trade Union Council; and the Workers' Beer Company.

72. Others included his son-in-law, 'Mr Walsh' and Henry Noble 'a friend of forty years' standing', *Daily Herald*, 15 February 1929.

73. Gatty, *op. cit.*

74. There is some confusion as to exactly what this badge was or whether it was sent personally by Lenin. Walshe says that he did get it from Lenin in 1922 and he 'was very proud of it'. Boyd suggests, 'Whether the medal was sent personally by Lenin or sent officially as a gesture of recognition and solidarity by the Russian CP or the Soviet Government is, however, another matter.' He points out that Lenin suffered his first stroke in May 1922. Boyd, *Jim Connell, op. cit.* p. 30.

75. *Daily Herald*, 15 February 1929.

76. James Connolly, *Songs of Freedom* (New York, 1907), a collection including 'The Red Flag' and republished as *The James Connolly Songbook* (Cork, 1977).

77. Walshe, *op. cit.* p. 97; and Boyd, *Jim Connell, op. cit.* pp. 20–1.
78. *Daily Herald*, 15 February 1929.
79. *Red Flag Rhymes.* The sentiments are reminiscent of those of another socialist songwriter, Joe Hill, who the night before he was executed in Salt Lake City, 19 November, 1915, wrote, 'Don't mourn for me—organise!' 'My Last Will' was his final poem: 'My will is easy to decide, For there is nothing to divide. My kin don't need to fuss and moan—'Moss does not cling to a rolling stone'. My body?— Oh! If I could chose, I would to ashes it reduce / And let the merry breezes blow / My dust to where some flowers grow / Perhaps some fading flower then / Would come to life and bloom again. / This is my last and final will./ Good luck to all of you, Joe Hill.'